ADULT AUTISM SUPPORT GUIDE

SIMPLE & EFFECTIVE STRATEGIES TO CREATE A SUPPORTIVE ENVIRONMENT, RECOGNIZE & UNDERSTAND SYMPTOMS, AND HELP AUTISTIC INDIVIDUALS BE HEARD

BY MAXINE KELLEY

CONTENTS

INTRODUCTION

> *"I think that it is not only autistic people who need to learn. The people who don't have autism must learn to understand us and be tolerant."*
>
> — PAUL MORRIS

In 1998, *Mercury Rising* was released in theaters. It stars Milo Hughes as nine-year-old boy Simon Lynch, who is an autistic savant who manages to crack a supposedly unbreakable cipher, and becomes marked for death by the NSA in order to keep the secret. Bruce Willis, the star of the movie, is FBI agent Art Jeffries, who tries to save young Simon from the wrath of Alec Baldwin's Nicholas Kudrow.

The movie's depiction of an autistic child was very stereotypical for its time, with some viewing it as a little insulting towards people with autism. While autistic savants are real, they are also rare, with a very rare few reaching the same levels as depicted in the movie. Contrary to how people with Autism Spectrum Disorder (ASD) have been portrayed in movies and other media, ASD can be a little more nuanced. Children eventually grow up to be adults, and ASD does not go away as one ages.

A study conducted by the Centers for Disease Control and Prevention (CDC) estimates that there are approximately 5.4 million adults in the United States with ASD —a little over 2.2% of the country's total population. In this study, approximately 4.3 million of those surveyed were men, while only an approximate 1 million were women. While this would indicate that men are more prone to being diagnosed with ASD than women, recent studies have shown that women are being under-diagnosed when it comes to autism.

While there is some science that indicates that the genetic differences between men and women are why more boys are diagnosed with autism than girls (at a rate of four to one in some cases) therapists and clinicians have come to realize that many girls and women who showed signs of ASD were misdiagnosed. This is because many of the tests and behavioral models used to identify ASD are based on boy's and men's behavioral patterns. While girls can show similar symptoms to boys, they can often be more muted. Because there was a previous misconception that autism was more common in boys than girls, the autistic traits of girls would often be dismissed or mislabelled.

Girls and women can also be more difficult to diagnose with ASD because they are better at "camouflaging" their autistic behavior. They are better at learning and imitating social behavior than boys, which allows them to hide or suppress their autistic traits. This behavior is often learned as an obligation in order to fit into society, and can have harmful effects for girls and women who continue to go undiagnosed—or worse, are misdiagnosed. Whether it is diagnosed early, or goes undiagnosed for years, life with ASD can be challenging not just for those living with it, but also for those around them.

According to the CDC, ASD is currently the fastest-growing developmental disability in the world. Those living with ASD also tend to have other co-occurring conditions, such as Attention Deficit Hyperactivity Disorder (ADHD), Obsessive Compulsive Disorder (OCD), anxiety, and depression. They are also more prone to serious conditions like epilepsy, digestive issues, or problems related to their metabolism. The extent of an autistic person's symptoms can also vary, meaning that no two autistic people are exactly alike in their autistic traits and symptoms.

Many adults show more "normal" behavior than what is often represented in the media. Having the condition formerly known as "high-functioning autism" (a term that is now seen as offensive to those with ASD), autistic people with mild ASD symptoms can often manage them to the point where they can live relatively normal lives. "Asperger's Syndrome" is another term that was used to describe high-functioning autism, and was an actual diagnosis for a form of autism until it was replaced with the ASD diagnosis in 2013. While Asperger's Syndrome is no longer used by clinicians, it is still used culturally, with some "aspies" (people diagnosed with Asperger's Syndrome) preferring to use that term rather than ASD.

YOU CAN'T BEAT AUTISM, BUT YOU CAN OVERCOME IT

ASD is a disorder that begins at conception. It causes the brain to develop fundamentally differently from that of a regular person. Because of this, there is and will never be a cure for autism.

While you may not have met someone with severe autistic traits, there is a very good chance you might know someone with less severe autism symptoms. In fact, many famous people, both throughout history and in our present time, have been diagnosed with autism, and you might not even have known it. Scientists like Albert Einstein and Henry Cavendish are believed to have been autistic to some extent. The co-founder of Microsoft, Bill Gates, is also thought to have autism based on some of his mannerisms and behaviors. Actor Anthony Hopkins is confirmed as having Asperger's Syndrome, as does entrepreneur Elon Musk, who famously announced it to the world when he hosted Saturday night live in May 2021.

But closer to home, it could be a family member, a friend, co-worker, or someone you see or deal with on a regular or semi-regular basis. If you are reading this book, you clearly have an interest in learning more about autism. Maybe you have a family member who is, or has recently been, diagnosed with autism. Or maybe the new hire at work is on the spectrum and requires special accommodations. Maybe a longtime friend recently revealed that they have Asperger's, but because they seem "normal" (or maybe "relatively normal" by your standards), the sudden admission has caught you off guard. Or maybe you merely suspect that someone you know may have autism, and don't know what to do.

How do I know? This book is the culmination of an over-fifteen-year journey. It first started when I realized that one of my coworkers was on the spectrum. She had tried to share with me her condition, but I didn't—couldn't—understand it at the time. It made me realize how little I knew about autism, and how difficult it was for autistic people as well. This would be the beginning of my passion—to help teach people about autism, and to help them better communicate with autistic people.

If you have found yourself lost and struggling to find your way in trying to learn about autism spectrum disorder, then you have come to a place of clarity and enlightenment. Within the pages of this book, we will show you what autism is: its symptoms, its traits, and its challenges. We will show you some of the daily struggles autistic people have to go through in their daily lives. And most importantly, we will show how you can help autistic people manage their symptoms, cope with their traits, and overcome the challenges they face.

1

THE NEURODIVERGENT AND THE NEUROTYPICAL

Have you ever stopped and wondered, "what is that person thinking?" I don't just mean the obvious, but more like, "what is going on inside their heads? What process made them come to that conclusion? Why did they think about that conclusion and not something else?" I do—all the time. More than I ever really want to, in fact. I have to, because sometimes, I really just don't get how people think the way they do.

People do that to me too: They look at me weird, or say that I'm crazy because of some of the things I say or do, like they can't understand how or why I am who I am. Makes sense I guess: I'm the one with Asperger's, and they're the "normal" ones.

W hile there are many clinical terms—and some slang terms that can be used to describe ASD —autism support communities have developed their own words and ideas to help not only to explain autism to others, but also to help make the collection of traits more accepted within society. As previously mentioned in the Introduction, terms like 'high-functioning' and 'low-functioning' autism are no longer the terms of choice.

NEUROTYPICAL VS. NEURODIVERGENT

- Within ASD and other mental support forums and communities, one might find words like "neurotypical" and "neurodivergent" used to describe people. While these are not considered to be official clinical terms, they are commonly used by those who deal with ASD.

Neurotypical

A neurotypical person is a person whose brain has developed normally based on the accepted standards of medical science and/or society. It represents the average person with no physical brain-related health issues or mental health issues. A neurotypical person is someone who:

- Has never needed cognitive or behavioral testing
- Had no speech-delay issues as a child
- Has met all of the standard development and behavioral milestones as a child and young adult
- Has no sensory issues
- Can learn new skills easily, and can adapt to change
- Can interact with others adequately

Most people are considered to be neurotypical. While it may seem odd to assign a word such as neurotypical to describe someone as "normal", it fits into the context of the other terms used by members of the autism community to describe ASD.

Neurodiversity and Neurodivergent Individuals

The idea of neurodiversity was created in 1998 by Australian sociologist Judy Singer. The idea behind neurodiversity is that everyone's brain develops in its own unique way. While all brains tend to develop in the same way, each brain is considered unique, and can have its own developmental quirks. Most of the quirks can be benign and harmless, while others can cause the brain to function or process information differently. Individuals with these types of brains are considered to be neurodivergent.

A person who is neurodivergent will face challenges in everyday life and society that neurotypical people will not. But neurodivergent people will also have strengths that they can lean into to help them offset their challenges. This can include a better memory, or the ability to process complex information like calculations in their head. Most neurodivergent people are strong visual and auditory learners, and are known to excel in subjects like math, science, and the arts.

While neurodivergent individuals are generally equated to people with ASD in this book, the term is not limited only to autism. A person is also considered to be neurodivergent if they have ADHD, down syndrome, dyslexia, social anxiety, tourette syndrome, and mental health conditions like bipolar disorder, OCD, and others.

The idea behind the neurodiversity concept is to support a more inclusive environment for people who are neurodivergent. Those who support these terms tend to believe that autism isn't a disease that needs to be cured, but rather a unique form of mental development that should be accepted. Even if one does not hold a similar view, the use of neurotypical, neurodiversity, and neurodivergent, is currently more acceptable language than previous terms used to describe people with ASD.

A CLOSER LOOK AT THE AUTISM SPECTRUM

Autism Spectrum Disorder is considered to be a neurological and developmental disorder. It is considered to be a developmental disorder because symptoms of ASD begin to appear in children within their first two years of life. However, ASD can be diagnosed at any point in a person's lifetime. This is because symptoms of ASD can be mild enough that they can be overlooked. This is particularly problematic with girls and women as we've already outlined.

The Diagnostic and Statistical Manual of Mental Disorders (DSM-5) describes people with ASD as often having difficulty interacting and communicating with others, restricted or limited interests, and repetitive behavior. These, along with other symptoms, can affect a person's ability to function at school, work, or in other aspects of daily life.

The reason autism is considered to be a spectrum disorder is because of the wide variety of symptoms a person with autism can experience. These symptoms can also vary in severity from person to person, so much so that no two people with ASD experience it in the exact same way. Some individuals with ASD require little in the way of support in order to live relatively normal lives, while others require daily or constant support in order to help manage their symptoms or to carry out basic tasks.

Signs and Symptoms of ASD

There are two primary categories of ASD symptoms one can look out for when dealing with someone who might have ASD. While no one person with ASD has all of these symptoms, most will have some from both categories. These particular symptoms are those commonly found in adults, and while some of these symptoms may be seen in autistic children, diagnosing children with ASD is a much different process, and focuses on other symptoms and developmental benchmarks.

The first category—social behaviors and communication—are less noticeable, as some could also be attributed to a person who is merely shy or socially awkward. These symptoms can include (National Institute of Mental Health, 2022):

- Difficulty making and maintaining eye contact, or avoiding it altogether
- Not looking at, or not appearing to listen to, the person speaking
- Doesn't always share interests, emotions, or enjoyment with others
- Is slow to respond, or does not respond to one's name or other verbal bids for attention
- Difficulties comprehending or following the verbal back and forth of a conversation
- A tone of voice that is sing-song, or flat and robot-like
- Difficulty understanding another person's point of view
- Difficulty predicting or understanding another person's actions
- Talking at length about a favorite subject without giving others a chance to respond, or not noticing when others are uninterested in the topic
- Making gestures, movements, and facial expressions that do not match what is being said
- Difficulties making friends
- Difficulties in adjusting to social situations

The second set of symptoms commonly seen in people with ASD involves repetitive or restrictive behavior. This can include (National Institute of Mental Health, 2022):

- Echolalia, the repetition of words and phrases
- Self-stimulatory behavior (stimming): repetitive and oftentimes unusual body movement, such as flapping one's hands, or rocking back and forth while sitting or standing still
- Intense and lasting interest in specific topics, like facts, numbers, or details
- Having overly focused interest in something, such as the moving parts of an object
- Having highly established routines, and becoming agitated or upset if those routines are disrupted
- Being more or less sensitive to sensory input than others

AUTISM AND THE BRAIN

The science behind autism, and our understanding of it is, while not necessarily in its infancy anymore, still far from complete. Because it is fundamentally a neurodevelopmental condition, autism's effect on the brain is key to understanding the condition. Unfortunately, despite a number of studies, no one characteristic has been found that can be used to easily identify autism traits in a neurodivergent brain. While the brain of each autistic person studied has shown unique variances in growth and formation, no unique pattern has yet to be found. But despite the lack of pattern, researchers have found common "trends" within these brains that might one day help to provide insight into understanding the autistic brain.

Through the use of Magnetic Resonance Imaging (MRI) scans, researchers have found that parts of the autistic brain can differ from those of neurotypical brains. Likewise, children who develop autism also develop differently from neurotypical children. Studies have shown that the brains of some children who are later on diagnosed with ASD grow at a much faster rate while in their infancy. This can sometimes lead to these children having enlarged heads and brains.

Normally, a neurotypical brain grows until it reaches adulthood, and starts to shrink as a person gets older. However, neurodivergent brains tend to start shrinking sooner, usually before their mid-twenties.

Neurodivergent people are also found to have an excess of cerebrospinal fluid surrounding their brain. This fluid surrounds the brain and spinal cord. This fluid is found in all people, and helps to clear waste, keep the brain buoyant, and even provides some protection to the brain from impacts to the head. However, people diagnosed with ASD are found to have much more cerebrospinal fluid in their heads as early as six months old, and persisting up to through the third year. This excess fluid can not only contribute to having an enlarged head, but also seems to be an indicator of the severity of autistic traits in later life, with those with the most excess fluid developing the most prominent traits.

The researchers have also noticed differences in the size of individual parts of the neurodivergent brain compared to the neurotypical brain.

- **Amygdala:** The part of the brain that deals with the processing of memories, emotional responses, and decision making. Researchers have found that the amygdala of autistic patients tends to be smaller than in neurotypical brains. However, this research is conflicted, as some research only points to the amygdala shrinking if the patient has anxiety. Other studies have also noted an increase in size of the amygdala during early development, with the size difference decreasing over time. Autistic girls also tend to have a more affected amygdala than boys, with studies showing that autistic girls with an enlarged amygdala have more severe emotional problems, including anxiety and depression.

- **Cerebellum:** Researchers have found that patients with ASD tend to have a decreased amount of brain tissue in the cerebellum. Primarily related to motor control, the cerebellum may also be involved with some other cognitive functions like emotional control, languages, and the ability to focus.

- **Cerebral Cortex:** The brain's outer layer, the cerebral cortex manages language, memory, thought, consciousness, perception, and awareness. In a neurotypical brain, the cerebral cortex tends to have a common thickness of around 2-4mm. However, researchers have found that in neurodivergent brains, the cortex has a different pattern of thickness, including a thinner temporal cortex and a thicker frontal cortex.

- **Corpus Callosum:** Located near the center of the brain, the corpus callosum is the white matter that connects the two hemispheres of the brain together. It also contains many of the connectors that reach out across the brain. Studies have found that people whose brains do not develop parts of the white matter are more likely to develop ASD.

- **Hippocampus:** While it is unclear if it persists into adulthood, autistic children, and adolescents diagnosed with autism, are often found to have an enlarged hippocampus. The hippocampus plays a major role in learning and memory.

What exactly these differences mean is still something being investigated by scientists and researchers. Individually, each change does not point directly to ASD. People with anxiety disorders, for example, often have a smaller than average amygdala. While a larger hippocampus can be correlated to better verbal learning and memory, how it impacts ASD is still a mystery. All researchers know for certain is that the neurodivergent brain is noticeably different from the neurotypical brain in terms of size and shape, but the how and the why of it are still very much a mystery.

Signs and Symptoms of ASD

Being a spectrum disorder, other disorders that were once thought to be unique were eventually linked to ASD, and are now under the umbrella of the ASD diagnosis. However, their original names are still often used.

Formerly known as a high-functioning form of autism, **Asperger's Syndrome** is a form of autism where the individual has difficulty with social skills, but otherwise appears to be neurotypical. They have trouble understanding social situations, and can often miss more subtle social cues, like innuendo, humor, and sarcasm. People with Asperger's tend to have rigid behaviors and thinking patterns that can be repetitive at times, and can be inflexible when forced to change such behaviors.

Officially, Asperger's syndrome is now part of the ASD diagnosis. However, many people diagnosed with Asperger's still prefer to use the term Asperger's when describing their condition, in part because of stereotypes towards ASD, and because of Asperger's portrayal in media.

A rare neurodevelopmental disorder, **Rett's Syndrome** occurs almost exclusively in girls, and is believed to mostly occur as a result of a mutation in the MECP2 gene. Rett's is a spectrum disorder with a number of variants, but all have similar base symptoms that are similar to the more standard autistic ones.

Childhood Disintegrative Disorder (CDD) is another disorder whose primary characteristic is the loss of previously learned skills. CDD usually presents after two or more years of normal development (normally around the 3-4 year mark) but can present anytime before the age of 10. Children with CDD lose a number of previously learned skills, including language and social skills. They can also lose motor functions and skills, including bowel and bladder control.

Another common autistic disorder, **Kanner's Syndrome** mostly affects the mental abilities of a person with the syndrome. Children with Kanner's have difficulty with language and in some cases even speaking, as well as difficulties with socializing. They can also show an obsession with objects.

Pervasive Developmental Disorder – Not Otherwise Specified (PDD-NOS), like Asperger's Syndrome, was previously defined as a subtype of autism before it was folded into the newer ASD diagnosis. PDD-NOS was previously used as a catch-all for forms of autism that did not conform to any of the other defined forms of autism.

WHAT IS NORMAL?

"Normal" can be a tricky thing. Normal is defined as something that occurs naturally; a tree grows in the ground, for example. Normal is also defined as the statistical average, such as that the majority of people are right-handed. In general, normal is considered to be whatever conforms to a standard, type, or regular pattern. But is being abnormal wrong? That is both a simple and complicated answer.

A tree cannot survive underwater. It requires oxygen and light, both of which tend to be in short supply when submerged. Most mammals, including humans, also cannot survive under water for long periods of time. Even if we have a steady supply of oxygen so that we don't outright drown, if we stay submerged for extended periods of time, it can begin to affect our body negatively. Trying to do so would be considered abnormal. But what about left-handed people? Are they abnormal? Technically, yes. Only around 10% of the world's population is left-handed, the rest being right-handed. But does the rest of the world see them as aberrations? Not really.

Being left-handed is not a choice. While the exact science is still being understood, being left-handed is thought to be related in part to genetics. But there is also a social aspect to it as well. If you have left-handed parents, you're more likely to be left-handed. But even then, right-handedness is still dominant among the global population. But does being left-handed mark you as being special in the eyes of others? Not generally. Because society has come to accept the quirk of being left-handed.

Normal can be seen in two ways: what is naturally normal, and what is socially normal. What is naturally normal is often backed up by science and other facts that are difficult to dispute. Going back to trees for example, a tree grows in the ground. We all know that trees cannot grow in water. But there are some tree species, like the bald cypress and the water tupelo, that can survive and even thrive in high levels of fresh water. They are the exceptions to the rule. Both types of trees have adapted to survive in swampy areas where flooding is common, where their roots spend most or all of their time in soil that is highly saturated, and contains little or no oxygen. Where other trees would die due to a lack of oxygen in the soil they are planted in, these two species of trees, along with several others, have adapted to their environment in order to over-come these obstacles. But compared to other trees, they are definitely not considered "normal".

Left-handed people can also be considered naturally abnormal because the majority of the population is predominantly right-handed. This can make things difficult for left-handed people, as most of the tools we use in everyday life, including simple things like note-books and scissors, are designed for right-handed people. But how often do you notice a left-handed person? Probably not very, even if you've seen one. That is because being left-handed is not something that is considered "abnormal" in our society.

Just because something is naturally abnormal, does not mean it is also socially abnormal. We all have unique quirks. Some of these quirks are more obvious than others. Stuttering, for example, is a quirk that is more noticeable. But while it may seem odd to you, it is not something that is usually highlighted. If a person has an issue with stuttering, it may seem odd at first, but soon enough, we just come to accept it as a quirk that person has. Overtime, some people may not even notice that person is stuttering at all. It's just something that person does, and they come to accept it to the point of almost ignoring it.

What people and society consider to be normal can change overtime. There is no one person or group who defines what should be considered normal and not. Even in the cases where something is initially considered abnormal, such concepts can be challenged, and eventually changed, to where the majority of society can come to accept what was once considered to be abnormal as the "new normal" or vice versa. Smoking, for example, used to be socially acceptable, but is now seen as something to avoid. Being part of the LGBTQ+

community, while still a ways from being accepted as normal, is still more accepted today than it was even just a few years ago.

A person's views, and through it, society's view, of what it considers to be normal and abnormal, can change over time through education, acceptance, and exposure to new ideas and concepts. But such change doesn't come spontaneously. Just because something different is presented to a person or to a society, it does not automatically mean that it will be accepted. More likely, it will be rejected, and either vilified or demeaned in order to maintain the status quo.

Tying it All Together

- A neurotypical individual is a person with no atypical brain function or structure, while a neurodivergent individual is a person with different brain functions and structures
- Neurodiversity is a concept where everyone's brain develops in its own unique way. It is a concept used to help promote inclusivity within the autism community
- People with autism have a variety of autistic traits and symptoms, many of which come in

different severities. Because of this, no two people with autism experience autism in the same way

- Autism can affect the growth and development of the brain, but we don't understand what this means or why yet
- Autism has a number of different types, including Asperger's, Rett's, and Kanner's Syndrome, as well as Child Disintegrative Disorder and Pervasive Developmental Disorder – Not Otherwise Specified
- ASD is not a disease or illness that can be cured; it is the result of a person's brain developing differently from others. For autistic people, autism is normal for them
- "Normal" can be subjective. What is naturally normal or abnormal is not always what is considered to be socially normal or abnormal

2

ABLEISM AND THE DRIVE TO CAMOUFLAGE

Carrie looks like your typical mother of two. She is happy and social, and is always there for her kids. At least, that's what everyone sees. They don't know she practices what to say in the mirror and to make sure she has the right look on her face. They don't know she has to focus on the bridge of a person's nose when she talks to them, because looking them in the eyes makes her nervous. Or how much focus it takes for her to not constantly fidget when she's out with her friends, or to keep up with conversations. She has to look "normal".

Carrie knows she has a problem. She's not sure what it is. It could be anything. But her boss hates disabled people, and refuses to deal with them. And her friend

Laura thinks she just has a low tolerance for alcohol and just needs to drink less. The only time she ever drinks is when she goes out with others. She tried to talk to her doctor about it, but she just said it was nerves, and maybe a bit of anxiety. Everyone's got that. But the pills she prescribed Carrie didn't help, and she just doesn't know what to do anymore, except to just grin and bear it.

Discrimination is a common issue in any society. Men have historically discriminated against women through misogyny. White people discriminate against people of color through racism. Straight people discriminate against LGBTQ+ through heterosexism. Likewise, neurotypical people discriminate against neurodivergent people through ableism.

WHAT IS ABLEISM?

Ableism is defined as discrimination or prejudice against individuals with disabilities. This can include both physical and mental disabilities. This is often based on the belief that the normal person is superior to a person with a disability. Like other -isms, ableism labels those with disabilities as being "less" than people without disabilities.

Ableism can come in many forms, and from all levels of society. It can be seen at the institutional level, where a given disability is seen as a problem that needs to be fixed or cured, and people with a disability are often overlooked because they are not considered capable of taking on a particular task or position. It can also affect how people are taught to look at a person with a disability, which in turn can affect how they interact with them.

At an interpersonal level, a person might follow beliefs taught at the institutional level, and might try to deal with a disabled person by trying to help them get "cured" of their condition. This can be particularly damaging to people with mental disabilities, as many mental disabilities cannot be cured. Symptoms can be treated and managed, but underlying conditions often-times cannot be "cured" in a way a layperson can understand, which can lead to misconceptions and conflict.

Ableism can also directly affect the disabled person themselves. Constant exposure to harmful messaging surrounding their disability can eventually be accepted either consciously or subconsciously. This can lead to other problems, such as low self-esteem and depression.

How people express ableism can vary. Being hostile towards a disabled person is not uncommon, either in the form of taunting or bullying. Others tend to take a more "benevolent" approach, where they view the disabled person as being weak and in need of rescuing. Oftentimes, these people think they are being good and helping, but they are actually belittling the disabled person by highlighting the unequal power dynamic between the two. There are also those who are more ambivalent towards the disabled, being both hostile and benevolent towards them at the same time.

What Ableism Looks Like

Signs of ableism in society can be both easy to spot out in the open, and more covert and hidden. Part of the problem with ableism is that not all disabilities are treated equally. People with more physical disabilities might earn more sympathy than those with mental or cognitive disabilities. Disabilities that are rare or uncommon will also face more ableism than those that are more common. Likewise, those disabilities that have a history of being stigmatized, like many mental disabilities, are more likely to be the subject of ableism.

At a more institutional level, ableism can be seen in the form of lack of accessibility in a building, refusing to provide reasonable accommodations for a disabled person, or segregating disabled people from regular people in school or work environments. It can also be seen in the way the staff treat people with disabilities, or in the material being taught at schools. Institutional ableism also includes disabled people being passed over for certain roles or positions, such as casting a non-disabled actor in the role of a disabled person. Media also has a habit of framing disabilities in tragic or inspirational ways that don't often reflect the reality of the person living with the disability, or make light of the person's experiences with the disability.

At a more personal level, people can show ableism in the way they talk and interact with a disabled person. Not considering a guest's disabilities when planning an event, or using a feature meant for disabled people when you are not disabled, are common examples. Treating a person inappropriately because they are disabled, like talking to a mentally disabled person like a child when they want to be treated like an adult, is another form of ableism. Not respecting the needs of others, such as wearing heavy scents in a scent-free zone, can also be considered ableism.

Even the words we use can display ableism. Ableist micro-aggression is when a person uses words or phrases to slight or insult a person based on some aspect of their being. Aside from a disability, it can also target a person's ethnicity, gender-identity, or even the part of the country they live in. Saying that someone doesn't look like they have a disability, or aren't disabled because they appear to act normally, is a form of ableism. Things like, "Are you off your meds?" and "Why are you acting so crazy today?", when directed at a disabled person, are not just insulting, but also ableism. Self-deprecating comments like "I'm very OCD when it comes to cleaning", or calling someone by a condition they do not have—"She's being very bipolar today"—are also considered ableism.

The Effects of Ableism

Though ableism towards disabled people can be common, in many cases it is not intended as such. There are of course people who are naturally hateful of others not like them, but oftentimes, particularly in the case of friends and family, the ableism they take part in is unintended. While they may have the best of intentions, lack of informed knowledge on disabilities can lead to misconceptions and incorrect assumptions about a disabled person, leading to ableism.

But whether it is intended or not, ableism does have very real, very negative, effects on disabled people, whether they are physically or mentally disabled.

- **Barriers in Healthcare:** Ableism in healthcare can make it difficult for people with disabilities to get help, or to get quality help. Because the person is disabled, medical practitioners will sometimes assume that the person has a lower quality of life than a non-disabled person. This can lead to symptoms of other health issues being ignored. This can also lead to the disregard of a disabled person's life. When faced with a choice, a doctor might choose to save the life of a non-disabled person over a disabled person. People with undiagnosed disabilities can also fear being diagnosed because of the potential repercussions such a diagnosis might come with. This can lead them to not seek help for other medical conditions as well.

- **Difficulties Finding Jobs:** People with ASD that have few supportive needs can not only live normal lives, but can also go on to earn college or other diplomas and degrees. However, as of 2018, 85% of autistic people with college degrees were unemployed (Autism Facts & Statistics, 2022). Overall, 75% of autistic adults are either unemployed or underemployed (Autism Facts & Statistics, 2022). Even if a disabled person is qualified (or even overqualified) for a position, employers are prone to hiring the non-disabled alternative either because they are unwilling to work with a disabled person, don't know how to accommodate a disabled person, or see the cost of accommodating a disabled person as being not worth the effort.

Eugenics

Eugenics is an erroneous scientific theory and set of fringe beliefs where, in order to improve the genetic stock of the human race, people with undesirable qualities, or people who are deemed inferior, are prevented from reproducing. By only allowing people with the optimal or ideal qualities to give birth to the next generation, it would remove less desired traits from the gene pool, and improve the overall genetic quality of the population.

The idea of selective breeding is not new. It is commonly used today with plants and animals to help weed out undesirable traits and qualities, or to create new traits in an existing organism. Unfortunately, when it comes to humans, eugenics and selective breeding often go hand-in-hand with racism and ableism. When eugenics was at its height in the early 20th century, governments put in place laws that ensured that their ideal candidates for the "perfect human" could have children, or in some cases even marry. Those who did not meet their criteria were not allowed. This often included the mentally disabled, people of color, and even criminals.

While people with disabilities were not the only target of eugenics, people with mental disabilities like ASD suffered greatly at the hands of eugenics. During World War II, the Nazi's, in order to fit the ideals of the "perfect man" outlined in *Mein Kampf*, segregated German society. Those who were "unfit" were either sterilized, institutionalized, or just killed en masse. Even after the war, eugenics was still used to carry out mass sterilization programs in the United States, some of which targeted people with mental disabilities.

Whether the concept of eugenics itself has any validity is not the point here. Historically, eugenics has been used as an excuse for one group to oppress another. Some of the concepts found in the -isms of today can trace their roots back to the principles of eugenics. And while modern eugenics focuses on the alteration of genes through genetic testing and engineering, it still raises the question of whether the eugenics of old might resurface in the new, modern form of eugenics.

CAMOUFLAGING

As we discussed in chapter 1, there are a myriad of symptoms of ASD that can be perceived by others. While not all of the symptoms immediately signal that a person has ASD, they can at the very least be a sign that something is wrong with the person. But some people —women in particular—learn to hide their autistic behavior, and can force themselves to act in a "normal" way.

Like how a chameleon can change its color to blend in with its surroundings, camouflaging is when a person with ASD learns to hide their autistic traits by mimicking socially accepted behavior. The autistic person learns tricks and even rehearses ways to appear normal to other people, essentially putting on a mask to hide their symptoms.

Hiding one's quirks or personality from others is nothing new. At some point in our lives, everyone has a need to put on a brave face, or deal with people or situations they may not like with a smile. As social creatures, there are times when we have to don our own camouflage when dealing with certain situations we may not want to deal with, either because we have to, or because we want to be more socially accepted. People with ASD who camouflage do something similar, but their camouflage is far more detailed and worn far more often.

Even those who have mild autistic traits can still find it difficult to socialize with others. This can be made more difficult by the way some people treat people with autism, particularly when ableism is involved. Even when ableism is not involved, some people are just uncomfortable dealing with a mentally disabled person. These barriers can limit what an autistic person can see and do in the world. This is why for some, camouflaging their autistic traits is a necessary part of their lives.

Women Camouflage More Than Men

As previously mentioned, men are diagnosed with ASD at a much higher rate than women, at a ratio of approximately four to one. While there are several potential reasons for this, recent studies have shown that women are much more adept at camouflaging their ASD symptoms than men.

While both men and women employ camouflage, women are thought to do so at a much higher rate and degree. This is partially because girls and women's autistic traits tend to be more subtle than those of boys and men. This along with a greater tendency to socialize and try to fit in, makes them more likely to use camouflaging strategies. Girls with a higher IQ and less severe autistic traits are also shown to be more successful in masking their ASD, to the point where they can go undiagnosed well into adulthood.

However, part of the reason women camouflaging is effective is because many of the tests used to determine if a person is autistic are based on men. While women do have many of the similar symptoms and autistic traits as men, their severity and presentation can be vastly different. For example, while autistic boys are more prone to being overactive and more inclined to misbehaving, autistic girls are more prone to appearing anxious and depressed.

How Camouflage Works

While there are a variety of techniques that an autistic person can use to camouflage their autistic traits, most of them fall into roughly three categories.

Compensation is when a person with ASD uses strategies and techniques to overcome difficulties they have in certain social situations. This is done by learning and practicing techniques used to make up for a lack of social skills. This can include:

- Learning behavior from movies, television, and other media
- Watching and copying the behavior of other people
- Practicing expressions and body language
- Repeating common phrases and tones
- The use of scripts or prepared questions

Masking uses strategies that hide autistic traits and behavior from others. This is done either by finding ways to mimic socially acceptable behavior, or by repressing autistic traits that are not socially accepted. This can include:

- Hiding or downplaying interest in subjects
- Forcing eye contact or focusing on parts of the face that mimic eye contact
- Suppressing stimming behaviors
- Internalizing social or sensory discomfort

Assimilation involves a more in-depth form of camouflage where the autistic person will use strategies to try and fit in social settings and situations. This often involves acting in ways the autistic person wouldn't normally act. In some ways, it is like putting on a persona that is opposite of how they normally are. This can include:

- Forcing oneself to interact with others
- Talking with strangers when one does not want to
- Pretending to be interested in topics they don't care about

Depending on which traits a person with ASD has, they will employ a variety of camouflaging techniques depending on the amount of socializing and interacting with others that they need to do.

The Consequences of Camouflaging

While many people with ASD (either consciously or unconsciously) find camouflaging a necessary part of daily life, it is not without its consequences.

Camouflaging isn't just hiding one's autistic traits. For many it's also putting on an act that isn't reflective of their true selves. This leads many people who camouflage to feel that they are not being their true selves, and give others unrealistic perceptions and expectations. Many who camouflage also say that keeping up the act is exhausting both physically and mentally. Exhaustion however, is the lesser issue that people with ASD face.

Because of the deception and the lack of being able to express one's true self, many autistic people who camouflage fall into depression and anxiety after camouflaging. One study also found that in order to cope with the stress generated by camouflaging, participants had suicidal thoughts, or practised self-harm, or turned to alcohol to help deal with the social pressures (Bradley et al., 2021). Since camouflaging is used primarily in socializing with others, some autistic adults reported that their success, or failure, to adequately camouflage also contributed to their depression. Camouflaging is also a risk marker for suicide among people with ASD.

COMBATING ABLEISM

It can be difficult for neurotypical people to understand just how ingrained ableism is in our society, even when confronted with a person with ASD or some similar disability. While ableism is not always intentional, it is very common. Small things like hogging the elevator when a person with a mobility impairment needs to use it, or using the handicapped restroom when there are other stalls available, are examples of everyday ableism at play.

It's important to combat ableism because it is the primary factor that forces many people with ASD to camouflage their autistic traits. The more ableism an autistic person encounters, the more they feel they must employ camouflage in order to be accepted by the social circles they move in, or face rejection and other potentially harmful consequences.

Combating ableism can be as simple as having some forethought and being informed about disabilities. While one doesn't need to know about every potential disability out there, if you regularly deal with a disabled person, learning a bit about their disability can help you better interact with that person. But regardless of the disability, here are a few things you can do to help combat ableism.

- **Don't be patronizing:** Even if you think a person has a mental disability, don't just assume that they can't understand you. Using baby talk when addressing a disabled person isn't just demeaning and insulting to them; it doesn't look good for you either. Also, if the disabled person is with someone, don't address them first. Speak to the disabled person as you would a normal person. If a correction needs to be made, let them make it.
- **Don't be invasive:** People are naturally curious; it's part of human nature to want to know more about things that catch our interest. However,

sometimes that curiosity can be unwelcome. People also have a tendency to assume that a disability is due to trauma. While some disabled people are not against talking about their disability, questions surrounding their disability are often uncomfortable, particularly when some people feel like they are entitled to an answer. If for any reason you absolutely must ask such questions, at least make an effort to be friendly and diplomatic about it, and don't start your conversations with them.

- **Be considerate:** Just because someone has a disability, doesn't mean they hate their disability, and wish they could be normal. Many people are born with a disability, and have known no other life. Don't assume a disabled person wishes they were normal. Likewise, try to avoid using such language that compares a disabled person to a normal person. Even if a disabled person were to use such language, don't automatically assume that it is okay for you to do so as well.

- **Be mindful of your words:** As we mentioned earlier in the chapter, ableism can often be seen (or more accurately, heard) in the words we speak. Ablest micro-aggression is perhaps the most common form of ableism, and the one that often goes the most unnoticed. Being mindful of language that can be offensive to a disabled person will go a long way to help treat a disabled person more like a normal person.

- **Not every disabled person wants to be inspirational:** Calling someone 'inspirational' can be a good thing, but there is a limit. When it comes to a disabled person, calling them inspirational can be a double-edged sword. Calling a disabled person inspirational for being able to carry out common tasks can be seen as condescending. Yes, disabled people face more challenges in their daily lives, but overcoming them doesn't mean they've accomplished some great task.

- **Disabled people just want to be treated like normal people:** Just because someone is disabled, does not mean they want to be treated differently. While some accommodations will have to be made, most disabled people just want to be treated like everyone else. Disabled people are still people, and you should treat them as you would a normal person, and not just as a person with a disability.

Normalizing the Workplace for Disabled People

Aside from having a more difficult time finding employment, disabled people face other challenges in the workplace. Disabled people are often paid less for doing the same job as non-disabled workers. People with disabilities—particularly physical disabilities or mental disabilities that have visual symptoms—often face discrimination during the interview process. Even when well-intended, employers and interviews often fall afoul of ableism and a lack of understanding about disabilities. Even employers who hire disabled people often do not provide a positive work environment for that person, both intentionally and unintentionally.

In order to combat ableism in the workplace, employers must be as inclusive to disabled people as they are when dealing with other affirmative action issues. Employers must also educate themselves more about people with disabilities, make a better effort to be more accommodating, and promote inclusivity among their staff.

Dealing With Ableism in the Classroom

When one thinks of disabilities in school, one might think about how some disabled children have to be put in special education classes or programs, and how they are often separated from the rest of the school population. While this can be necessary for children with developmental disorders, many schools also have systemic ableism deeply rooted in how they operate. This can lead to a gatekeeping mentality, where those in a position to make changes to accommodate disabled people will choose not to do so based on either their own beliefs, or just because of a "that's not how we do things here" mentality.

In order to combat ableism in the classroom, educators must be better informed about their disabled students and their needs. Teachers make accommodations for their students all the time, and accommodating disabled students is not that much different, so long as they understand the challenges a disabled student faces.

Inclusivity must also be practiced, both in the classroom and in the material being taught. This can include using educational material with a more inclusive range of characters, having disabled people come to the class, or even hosting special events designed to accommodate disabled students. This will not only help the disabled student fit in, it can also be beneficial for non-disabled students. Working and learning alongside students of different backgrounds and abilities can be enriching and help better prepare students for the future, as well as helping combat ableism in the next generation.

Tying it All Together

- Ableism is the discrimination and prejudice towards disabled people
- Ableism is more common towards people who don't look disabled, such as if they have a mental disability
- Ableism is not only seen in actions and how we consider disabled people, but also in the way we talk to them through ableist microaggressions
- Ableism can make it hard for disabled people to not only fit into society, but also to find jobs and get proper healthcare, including proper medical diagnosis
- Camouflaging is when autistic people use various strategies and tricks to appear normal by hiding their autistic traits and symptoms
- Camouflaging is a combination of compensating, masking, and assimilation
- Camouflaging is physically and mentally taxing to carry out, and can have long term

repercussions including anxiety, depression, and suicidal thoughts

- Being inclusive, considerate, and mindful of your words and language used towards disabled people can help combat ableism
- Affirmative action, equality, and educating employers and co-workers about disabilities can help combat ableism in the workplace
- Teachers and others in education also need to be properly educated about disabilities, and be more inclusive, in order to prevent a gatekeeping mentality and ableism in the school setting

3

THE EIGHT SENSES

*Carl hates noise. Everything is always so loud. Even
in his apartment, he has to wear his special headphones sometimes just so the noise coming from
outside his window doesn't drive him nuts. All the
honking and the sounds of cars and trucks going by
scare him sometimes, even at night when it should be
quiet. Sometimes it gets so bad he has to go and stuff
his head under his pillow (while he's still wearing his
headphones) just to enjoy some peace and quiet.*

*Work at least used to be quiet, but now the new guy is
sitting across from him, and he likes loud, heavy
music. He wears earphones when he listens to it, but
Carl can hear the music through them. He doesn't like
heavy metal, and the sound is distracting. He can't*

focus, he can't think, and all he wants to do is yell at
the new guy to turn the damn music off.

I f you were to ask the average person how many senses you have, you will most likely get an answer of five: sight, hearing, touch, taste, and smell. This is technically accurate. These are the five senses that we primarily use when dealing with the world around us. But are they the only senses we have? No, they are not. Exactly how many senses we have greatly depends on what your definition of a sense is. In the case of the first five, these are all "external" senses. But within our body, we have many more.

SO, THERE'S MORE THAN FIVE?

The exact number of senses we have is still a topic that is being researched, and is sometimes hotly debated. Currently, there are eight commonly accepted senses that have been identified by science, but that number is likely to rise as research continues into the subject. Aside from the five we all know, there are three others that most people are not aware of: vestibular, proprioceptive, and introspective.

Most of our senses work either through the use of specific body parts (like the eyes and ears), or through special receptor cells within other body parts.

Receptors in our skin, for example, give us our sense of touch, while receptors in our mouth, tongue, and throat give us our sense of taste.

The Five You May Know

- **Hearing (auditory input):** Our ability to hear lets us perceive the sounds around us, and filter them so we can tell which are important and which are not. This can include things like voices, music, car horns, or doorbells.
- **Sight (visual input):** Perhaps our most important sense is the ability to see through our eyes. It allows us to perceive the world around us and do things like read books, watch videos, or move about without bumping into things.
- **Smell (olfactory input):** The sensory receptors in our nose helps us better perceive the world around us. Not only can our sense of smell alert us to potential dangers or when something is otherwise wrong, it can also be used to help enjoy things like flowers and foods.
- **Taste (gustatory input):** Our sense of taste lets us perceive how something we eat tastes. Taste and smell are often closely linked, as we will often not eat something that smells questionable or bad.

- **Touch (tactile input):** Our sense of touch not only lets us perceive when something comes in contact with our body, but can also determine pressure, texture, temperature, and whether it causes us pain. Your sense of touch also plays an important role in bonding with others and in relationships.

The Three You May Not Know

Part of the reason these three senses are not commonly known is because they are for the most part internal to the body. Unlike the five we know, these three are used automatically by the body, and are not something we normally perceive unless we really stop to think about it.

- **Balance (vestibular input):** Your balance receptors are located in the inner ear, and as the name suggests, they help keep you balanced and upright. It also acts as a sort of internal GPS for your body, keeping track of gravity and our sense of body position among other things.
- **Internal (introspective input):** Often called the hidden sense, our internal sense tells us things about our body. Are we thirsty, or hungry? Do we need to go to the bathroom? It

also lets you feel other things about your body; when you are excited or scared, you can feel your heart beat faster and your pulse quicken.

- **Movement (proprioceptive input):** The sensory receptors for this sense are located in our muscles, joints, and tendons. This sense simply tells you where your body parts are without having to look at them.

SENSORY OVERLOAD IN NEURODIVERSE PEOPLE

In a neurotypical person, if we encounter excessive sensations and stimuli, we normally either do something to reduce the stimuli, or we distance ourselves from the stimuli. If the music we are listening to is too loud, we turn it down. If something is too hot or too cold, we set it down. While this may seem simple and straightforward for a neurotypical individual, it is not always so for the neurodivergent.

Neurodiverse people can often have a condition called Sensory Processing Disorder (SPD), more commonly known as sensory overload. Sensory overload occurs when the brain receives more sensory input than it can handle. When such overloads occur, they can cause the person to be overwhelmed, which can lead them to react negatively.

SPD comes in two forms: hypersensitivity and hyposensitivity. People who are hypersensitive are more susceptible to environmental stimuli, while people who are hyposensitive are less sensitive. The extent of sensitivity (or lack thereof) varies from person to person, but can reach extremes where hypersensitive people experience sensations normal people do not. Likewise, hyposensitive people can risk harming themselves through their lack of sensation.

The causes of sensory overload vary from person to person. SPD, while a common trait in autistic people, can also be present in people diagnosed with ADHD, Post-Traumatic Stress Disorder (PTSD), and some other developmental or psychiatric disorders. The causes and triggers of sensory overload can vary greatly depending on the condition a person has. Because of this, the causes of SPD are poorly understood, and still being studied.

Sensory overload can trigger a number of symptoms in a person. This can include (Rudy, 2021):

- Anxiety and fear
- Restlessness
- Irritability or anger
- Overexcitement
- Muscle tension

- Increased heart rate
- Rapid breathing
- Extreme sweating
- Covering the ears or eyes to block out stimulus
- Not wanting to be touched or approached
- Stimming or self-harming behavior

Aside from these symptoms, people with ASD can also go into a meltdown. Often viewed as a "tantrum", meltdowns are in actuality an intense response to sensory overload. During a meltdown, a neurodivergent person can lose control of their behavior and emotions. Unlike tantrums, which are more common during the childhood years, adults with ASD can experience meltdowns. And while they may seem sudden, and an overreaction, to neurotypical people, they are in fact the most aggressive symptom of sensory overload.

Hyposensitivity

While hypersensitivity may seem more common when dealing with people diagnosed with ASD, hyposensitivity can still be present. As we mentioned in the previous section, hyposensitivity is the lack of sensory input from at least one of the senses. This is in some ways more dangerous than hypersensitivity, because the lack of sensory input can lead to injury.

Identifying dangers, and things that could do us harm, is often done through our senses. We might know a pot of boiling water is hot, but we won't know if it's too hot until we put our hand close enough to the pot to feel the heat radiating from it. A person who has hyposensitive tactile sense might need to touch the pot before they can tell if it's hot or not—or, in a more extreme case, they might grab the pot and burn themselves, without even realizing it.

Because people with hyposensitivity require higher sensory inputs in order to sense anything, they often tend towards extremes. They may want bright lights, loud music, or spicy food and strong smells, just so they can sense something. People with hyposensitive tactile senses can also be overly aggressive when touching things or people. This can be seen as rude or bullying, but in reality, the person is just trying to feel. And just like hypersensitive people, hyposensitive people can have the symptoms of sensory overload even when their senses are under-stimulated.

PREVENTING AND DEALING WITH SENSORY OVERLOAD

Sensory-Friendly Environments

Sensory overload does not generally happen out of the blue. While it is possible for sudden intense stimuli—like a loud sound or a strong smell—to suddenly appear and overwhelm an autistic person, most incidents of sensory overload are not instantaneous. When faced with increased sensory input, an autistic person will try to cope on their own before symptoms start to show up. If symptoms are ignored, or action is not taken in time, the situation could progress to the point of a meltdown. In order to avoid sensory overload, the areas where an autistic person normally works and resides must be set up to prevent any over-stimulation. These areas are known as sensory-friendly environments.

A common sensory-friendly environment you might not have thought about, regarding people with ASD, are scent-free zones. Scent-free zones are not just for people with ASD. People who are naturally hypersensitive to scents, as well as people with allergies, asthma, and some other medical conditions, can also have negative reactions to strong scents like perfume and cologne, or foods like shellfish. Autistic people with hypersensitive senses of smell also benefit from these environments, even if they were not designed for them in particular.

Creating a sensory-friendly environment does not often require a great undertaking. Sometimes, small changes to an environment can go a long way to helping a person. However, before you go about trying to make a sensory-friendly environment for someone with ASD, talk to them first. Get their input, find out what works and does not work for them, and adjust accordingly. Involving them in the process can go a long way to help build confidence in their environment and put them at ease. Some things to consider are:

- **Light and color:** People with visual hypersensitivity can find bright light distracting or even painful. Fluorescent lighting can also be problematic to some autistic people. Certain patterns can also be distracting to autistic people, and certain colors can have more profound effects on some. Red and yellow, for example, have long wavelengths, and can be stimulating to people with hypersensitive vision, while blue, which has a much shorter wavelength, can be more calming.

- **Clutter and movement:** Clutter can be difficult or necessary in several ways depending on an autistic person's sensitivity. Too much clutter can be distracting to some individuals, while a more minimalist space can also be just as distracting if there is not enough detail for the autistic person to focus on. If they have mobility or tactile issues, clutter can be a frustrating obstacle, or even dangerous if the autistic person is not paying attention. Some autistic people can also have issues moving around on smooth surfaces because of balance issues. Having things like hand rails, grab bars, and properly secured rugs can help an autistic person move about more confidently.

- **Sounds:** Autistic people can have issues not just with the volume of sound, but also the number of sounds present. Some can have difficulty separating the different sounds they hear, which makes it hard to focus on a particular sound, like the voice of an individual person speaking. Depending on how sensitive they are to sound generally, the problems they face can range from processing the sounds of traffic coming from an outside window, to the sound of a person typing down the hall, or even the ticking of a wall-mounted clock. Aside from potentially lowering the total amount, and accumulative volume, of sound in the environment, providing sound-blocking aids like earplugs or noise-canceling headphones can also do the trick.

- **Textures and Touch:** Autistic people, particularly those with tactile hypersensitivity, often do not like being touched unless they are in control of the touch. They can also sometimes require touch-related things that have different textures, either as part of stimming or if their tactile senses are hyposensitive. Be mindful of what materials and textures an autistic person comes in contact with, as well as providing items with different textures and tactile feeling if needed.

- **Scents:** As we've already shown, scent free zones are an excellent way to help an autistic person with a hypersensitive sense of smell. However, instead of going scent free, just removing specific scents that an autistic person can find triggering or uncomfortable (such as certain cleaning products, foods, and perfume) can help to create a sensory-friendly environment without getting rid of strong scents altogether.

- **Space:** if an autistic person has issues with balance or space, they may need to have a certain amount of empty space around them—whether it is more or less—in order to keep from being disoriented.

- **Taste:** A smaller issue—but one can be just as important nonetheless—is if the autistic person is in an environment that serves or deals with food. Certain flavors and textures can be uncomfortable for an autistic person to eat or drink. This can be different from foods they simply do not like. An autistic person may not like the taste of certain breads for example, but might still eat them if necessary. A person with hypersensitive taste however, may not like certain breads because the texture of the bread can be like sandpaper in their mouth. Likewise, if something is only mildly spicy to a neurotypical person, it may seem very spicy and have a strong—maybe even unbearable—flavor to an autistic person.

Coping With Sensory Overload

Regardless of whether or not a person with ASD is in a sensory-friendly environment, sensory overload is often inevitable. While it is ultimately up to the autistic person to deal with the sensory overload, there are ways you can help provide support. If you know a person has SPD, you can help by:

- **Talking and listening:** If an autistic person confides in you about their struggle with a particular event or situation, listen to them and be supportive. Being supportive can go a long way with helping them cope.
- **Know what to expect:** Understanding an autistic person's triggers and symptoms can help you not only better react, but help you better help them cope when they do appear.
- **Watch for triggers and symptoms:** Sometimes, you can spot triggers or see the symptoms of sensory overload beginning to manifest before an autistic person does. It could be because they are distracted, they are focused on something else, or they are just trying to grin and bear it. If you see something, let them know—the sooner the better.
- **Have a strategy:** If possible, work with the autistic person on a per-event strategy, or have an exit strategy should things go wrong. This can include having a plan if you know there are going to be triggers, or trying to find alternate

locations in order to avoid those triggers altogether.

If you are with an autistic person when they are having a bout of sensory overload, there are things you can do to help them cope.

- **Remain calm:** If the person you are with starts to show symptoms, or worse, has a meltdown, remain calm. If the person you are with starts to, for lack of a better term, "freak out", you also freaking out will not help the situation. Do your best to remain calm and supportive.
- **Try to reduce the offending sensory input:** If you know what triggered the symptoms of the overload, do what you can to try to lower the amount of input the autistic person is getting. This can include things like turning down the music, moving to another room, or removing the source of an offending smell. Also try to limit the amount of interaction the autistic person is having. Too many people clustering around an autistic person asking them what is wrong and how they can help can do more harm than good.
- **Protect them from harm:** If the autistic person starts to experience physical symptoms such as

stimming, do your best to make sure they do not put themselves in danger or harm themselves. While you might not be able to stop the symptom, you can ensure that the autistic person does not come to harm by moving potentially dangerous items and objects out of their reach, or by helping to minimize the danger by giving them something else to focus on.

- **Don't be forceful:** While there are some medications that can help counter some of the symptoms of sensory overload in the moment, such as anxiety, do not force them on the autistic person. Also, do not force any particular coping method or strategy on them that they do not want, or are not receptive to. Make the offer or the suggestion, but let them take the lead in dealing with their symptoms whenever possible. Trying to force something on them can not only make things worse, but also cause an autistic person to distrust you in the long run.

- **Give them time and space:** Sometimes, there is little you can do to help an autistic person in coping with their symptoms or dealing with a meltdown. Once you've done what you can, all that is left is to wait and ride it out. Trying to speed up or alter the recovery process can prolong the incident.

Tying It All Together

- Human beings have eight recognized senses: hearing, sight, smell, taste, touch, balance, internal, and movement. Scientists suspect that we might have many more
- Many people with ASD are either hypersensitive (more susceptible to stimuli), or hyposensitive (less susceptible to stimuli). These are known as Sensory Processing Disorders (SPD), also known as sensory overload
- Autistic people with SPD first start to show symptoms such as anxiety, restlessness, rapid breathing, and aversion actions. In the worst cases, they can have meltdowns
- Sensory-friendly environments are areas that have been adapted to prevent an autistic person from experiencing sensory overload
- You can help an autistic person deal with sensory overload beforehand by understanding their symptoms, forming a plan to try and help

prevent sensory overload, or planning how to deal with it when it occurs

- When a sensory overload occurs, you can help an autistic person through the incident by remaining calm, being supportive by trying to reduce the offending sensory input, and by giving them space when needed

4

COMMUNICATION BREAKDOWN

*Talking to people is hard. Dale hates it with a passion,
and it's frustrating. He likes being around people. He's
a good listener. He spent a summer in highschool
going door to door doing surveys, and it was one of
the highlights of his childhood. But while he's good at
listening to people, he has a hard time talking to them.
It's not that he's ineloquent or rude. Things can get
scrambled when they go from his brain to his mouth.
It's frustrating.*

*But it gets worse sometimes. When he's stressed, like
in a crowded place, it feels like the walls are closing in
on him. Like everyone's trying to get so close to him
that they're trying to crush him. When it's too loud
and noisy, or when there are just too many people, it*

freaks him out. And when he gets freaked out, his voice goes away. He'll either make strange sounds when he tries to talk, or nothing comes out at all. His doctor says it's just anxiety. Dale isn't so sure, but, whatever it is, it's really frustrating.

L anguage plays an important role in any society. If we cannot effectively communicate with one another, we cannot convey thoughts, ideas, or instructions, to name a few things. Language isn't just spoken. It's also the written word, and the symbols we use. Even emojis, which are not considered to be a language because they lack grammar, play an important role for younger generations who communicate through the internet.

Many mental disorders can affect the way a neurodivergent person speaks and understands language. People with ASD often have trouble speaking or understanding others when they speak. While there are ways to overcome this obstacle, one must first have an understanding of how language works for neurodiverse people.

Any language can be broken down into two basic forms: receptive language, and expressive language. Both are key, as you cannot have one without the other. A neurotypical person generally has no problems with either parts of the language, and can use both naturally, oftentimes without thinking. A neurodivergent person, on the other hand, might have problems using one or both parts of a language, which can present a barrier in both understanding and communicating with others.

TWO TYPES OF LANGUAGE

In simple terms, when learning a language there are two fundamental parts of the language that you need to learn: the vocabulary and the grammar. Learning a language's vocabulary allows you to speak that language. Learning the grammar of the language allows you to effectively communicate in that language. Just knowing the words "open" and "door" might get your point across, but you don't sound particularly intelligent when doing so. Likewise, knowing the proper grammar to go with a specific language won't be very helpful if you don't know any of the words in that language.

When using a language to speak with others, it can also be broken down into two parts. Receptive language (also known as listening language) is the language and associated skills we use to understand both verbal and non-verbal language. Expressive language is our ability to get our thoughts, needs, and wants out in a way that others understand. Language Processing Disorder is a mental condition where a person has trouble with either receptive or expressive language skills, or a combination of both. It is commonly seen not only in people with ASD, but also people diagnosed with other mental disorders and syndromes, such as epilepsy and Down Syndrome.

Receptive Language

Receptive language is essentially our ability to process and understand language. Receptive language skills allow us to understand what we are being told, whether it is following instructions or being asked a question. Receptive language skills are also key to understanding non-verbal communication, like hand-gestures and reading.

Neurodivergent people who have deficiencies in their receptive language skills have a hard time understanding things like jokes and nuance. They tend to take things they are told very literally. They can also have a hard time following conversations or answering questions about topics that were just discussed. They can also appear disinterested in conversations, even when they are not.

People with receptive language deficiencies also have difficulties following multi-step instructions, as well as verbal instructions. They can also misinterpret friendly conversations as being rude or confusing. Lack of receptive language skills can also be why some people with ASD don't always react to their own name when being called.

Expressive Language

If receptive language is the way we input information from others, expressive language is the way we output our language to others. Expressive language, and the associated skills, are what we use to communicate our thoughts, feelings, needs, and wants to others. Aside from language, this can also include gestures, the written word, and other signs and symbols.

Neurodivergent people who have trouble with expressive language find it hard to effectively communicate with others. They will have trouble choosing the correct words, and will use substitute words that are similar or sometimes even make up words in their place. They can also have trouble forming proper sentences. They can also have trouble speaking words, using incorrect tones and sounds when saying words.

People with expressive language deficiencies can often be anxious when speaking to others. Even if they know the answer or what to say, their issues with expressive language can make it difficult for them to express it, in turn making it difficult for them to keep up with conversations.

THE DIFFICULTIES COMMUNICATING WITH ASD

When language processing disorder is combined with the other autistic traits people with ASD have, it can make it very difficult for them to communicate with others. Aside from issues with receptive and expressive language, people with ASD can have other problems when communicating with neurotypical people:

- **Predicting and Interpreting Behavior:** By now it should be clear that the autistic mind works very differently than the neurotypical mind. Because of this, it is very difficult for neurodivergent people to predict and interpret the behavior and actions of others. In short, they literally cannot "put themselves in someone else's shoes", because their mind literally doesn't work like anyone else's.
- **Pragmatics:** Pragmatics refer to the proper use of language in social situations. This can include what tone of voice to use when, taking turns in a conversation, asking the appropriate

questions, or even when to talk to someone at all or not.

- **Interrupting:** Somewhat of an extension of pragmatics, some people with ASD have difficulties knowing when to speak and when not to speak during a conversation. This can be because they don't have the skills to understand when a person has stopped talking, or because they feel the need to interrupt because they don't want to miss out on being involved in the conversation.

- **Prosody:** Language isn't just words. It's also tone, tempo, and rhythm, collectively known as prosody. Autistic people often have problems both understanding and using prosody when they speak. This can result in them having a "flat" sounding voice. This can also be misinterpreted as showing lack of engagement or interest, humor, intelligence, or even a lack of emotional response.

- **Literal Thinking:** People with ASD tend to take things that they are told very literally. Colloquial sayings in particular can be confusing to them, as they may understand the saying in formal language, but not what the saying means colloquially.

It should be noted that not all autistic people will have all of these problems. People with ASD who require less daily support will have less trouble communicating than someone who needs more daily support. As with many things involving ASD, everyone is different, and has different challenges.

COMMUNICATING WITH SOMEONE ON THE SPECTRUM

Because people with autistic traits face many challenges, some are more difficult to interact with than others. If they have Asperger's Syndrome, or have less pronounced autistic traits, they can generally interact with others in a more normal way. However, if their autistic traits are more pronounced, and they have trouble communicating with others, there are ways you can help make conversations easier. As always, keep in mind that every person with ASD is different, and each has different traits and challenges. Here are some common things you can do to help keep a conversation on track.

- **Be patient:** If you are dealing with an autistic person that has more serious challenges when it comes to speech and social interaction, be patient with them. Don't expect quick answers, and take your time to explain instructions.

- **Be nice:** Be nice to an autistic person when you are speaking with them. They are not trying to be difficult on purpose. Don't be mean or condescending, and try not to treat the autistic person like a child. This is especially true when giving them directions and instructions.

- **Make sure you have their attention:** Some people with ASD have issues focusing, and their minds can sometimes wander. Make sure you have and keep their attention when you talk with them. Use their name when you address them, so that they know you are talking to them. Make sure you still have their attention when you ask them a question or give them instructions. Including things in the conversation that interest them, like hobbies, can also help them stay focused on the conversation.

- **Be clear:** Avoid using any confusing language, and avoid using idioms and colloquialisms. Sarcasm should also be avoided, as it could be taken literally. If you have to use any of these, make sure you explain to the autistic person what they really mean in order to avoid confusion.

- **Help them process information:** If the autistic person has trouble filtering out information, keep your sentences short, and say them slowly, pausing between words if necessary in order to let them keep up. Avoid using non-verbal communication like hand gestures and body language, as they can be either confusing or not picked up at all. Also be mindful of the environment you are both in, as there could be sensory input that might distract the autistic person. Using visual aids, such as symbols or graphs, can also help the autistic person understand and follow the conversation more effectively.

- **Avoid open-ended questions:** Ambiguous and open-ended questions can confuse an autistic person. When asking them questions, keeping them short and to the point can help them answer them more effectively. Structuring your questions can also help them better understand. Instead of asking something more ambiguous like "how was your trip?", instead ask things like "How was the drive?", "Did you go to the museum?", etc.

- **Listen Carefully:** When there is a misunderstanding, an autistic person won't usually pick up on it right away. Pay attention to what they are saying, and if they are misunderstanding something, or veering off topic, try to correct them and get them back on track.

- **Using other words instead of 'no':** "No" can be very ambiguous to an autistic person, and it can confuse them. When talking with an autistic person, only use "no" when absolutely necessary. Otherwise, try using other words or symbols, and explain why the autistic person can't do the thing being stopped or rejected.

- **Offer other ways to ask for help:** If an autistic person has difficulties speaking, or has trouble asking for help verbally, offer them other ways to communicate things. Tools like visual help cards, or even just texting or emailing can also be used to help them communicate more effectively.

Tying It All Together

- Communication can be broken down into two parts: receptive language, (the ability to receive and understand input) and expressive language

(being the ability to communicate ideas to others)

- Depending on their autistic traits, people with autism can have trouble understanding others. This can include trouble predicting and interpreting behavior, taking things too literally, interrupting, and even understanding the pragmatics and prosody of language
- When communicating with an autistic person, be patient and nice to them
- When communicating with people on the spectrum, make sure you are clear and avoid using ambiguous, open-ended language
- If an autistic person has issues communicating verbally, offer alternatives like texting, email, gestures, or visual cue cards

BUILDING A WORLD WHERE AUTISM IS UNDERSTOOD

"To measure the success of our societies, we should examine how well those with different abilities, including persons with autism, are integrated as full and valued members."

— SECRETARY GENERAL BAN KI-MOON

As I mentioned at the beginning of our journey together, my interest in researching autism and teaching people about how to communicate with those who have it began when I realized how little I understood myself. This isn't something I feel any shame about – it simply indicated that I needed to educate myself, and it ignited a passion for educating other people.

The media presents a very narrow view of what it's like to live with autism, and through no fault of our own, many of us simply don't understand the condition or what life's like for those who have it. I want to change that – both for the sake of people who have autism and those who don't – because the vast majority of us *want* to understand.

I know you're on the same page because you wouldn't be reading this book if you weren't... and I'd like to ask for your help in getting this information out to more people. Don't worry – it won't take much of your time. All I'd like you to do is leave a short review.

By leaving a review of this book on Amazon, you'll show other people who want to understand more about autism where they can find everything they need to know.

Simply by telling new readers how this book has helped you and what they can expect to find inside, you'll point them in the direction of the understanding they're looking for so they can communicate better with the autistic people in their lives.

Thank you for your support. The world is set up for neurotypical people, and as such, life can be very difficult for those who don't fit into the box. But by sharing this information and spreading understanding, we can help change that.

Scan the QR code to leave a quick review.

5

MENTAL HEALTH MATTERS

Laura is weird. She knows it, her family knows it, her friends (the few she has that aren't from an online chat room) know it. She has a high IQ, had a 3.9 GPA in school, but barely scrapes by on a part time job she does on her computer from home. Laura's parents think she's lazy, and a bit of a slob because she always wears the same three outfits. They've tried to encourage her, and even threatened to cut her off of all contact a few times, something they came to regret in the long run. But when they noticed that Laura was depressed, they convinced her to get help.

To everyone's surprise, Laura was diagnosed with autism spectrum disorder. But now in her late thirties, there was little the doctor could do. "You seem to be doing fine," he told Laura. "It looks like you've got that part figured out." He gave her a prescription for the depression, and a web address for an autism support group. Her parents were shocked at the total lack of care. But before they could do anything, a few days later, they got a call from the hospital...

L iving with ASD can be difficult, even for those who do not require much support in order to live a relatively normal life. Even though they are already considered to be living with a mental disability, autistic people must also look after their own mental health, and are just as susceptible to depression and other disorders and illnesses—in some cases, more so—than a neurotypical individual.

LIVING IN A NEUROTYPICAL WORLD

Modern society was not designed for the neurodivergent. Almost everything in our world is based on the neurotypical, and is thus designed for the neurotypical. A neurodivergent person trying to live in the neurotypical world can find it hard, tiring, and sometimes painful. Even autistic people who need little daily support, such as people with Asperger's Syndrome, can have a hard time adjusting to life among neurotypical people.

Perhaps the biggest issue autistic people face is being overstimulated in public areas, and not just busy places like subways, elevators, or restaurants. Even a street during a slow period of the day can be imposing to an autistic person. You have people moving about that you are trying to avoid running into while they do the same. Cars going by, sometimes honking their horns or have music blaring out their windows.

Quiet places that suddenly get loud and busy can also be jarring. One minute, they are sitting in the corner of a quiet coffee shop trying to focus, and a gaggle of loud people suddenly sit down at the table next to them. For an autistic person with hypersensitivity, this can be going from a proverbially calm sea to suddenly being in the middle of a chaotic storm. Sensory overload can quickly build up and symptoms can begin to appear, forcing an autistic person into a flight or fight response before a meltdown occurs.

This sort of sensory overload, in places where the neurotypical would not face similar issues, can also lead to information overload. As we discussed in the previous chapter, communicating with an autistic person can be a challenge in and of itself. But trying to have that conversation in a non-sensory-friendly environment, like many places in the neurotypical world, can make it even more challenging. Background noises can make it hard for them to hear what a person is saying, while a constantly changing environment—like people walking around and talking to others—can take attention away from the task at hand. If the person they are speaking to isn't communicating in a neurodivergent-friendly way, just trying to keep up with conversation can also be trying.

Because information overload can confuse an autistic person, it can result in them saying or doing confusing things as they try to process the information. Many autistic people will have prepared scripts in their heads regarding how to respond to questions or what to say in certain situations. But if they are taken off-script or become confused, they might muddle things, or start to show frustration or symptoms of sensory overload.

Clothing can also be an issue for autistic people with hypersensitive tactile sense. Many will only have a few shirts and or other pieces of clothing they will wear all the time, as other garments can feel itchy or, in rare cases, even be painful to wear. While some autistic people will try to get creative with this limited wardrobe, others will not, and will always seem to wear the same things. This can make them stand out more in a crowd, making them further uncomfortable.

In order to cope with their autistic traits, autistic people often have specific routines in their daily lives that they follow. These routines can often be strict and unyielding, because to do otherwise is to invite confusion and hardship. Neurotypical people don't understand this inflexibility because, in many instances, an autistic person simply cannot be flexible. They either don't know how to be, or can't afford to be, flexible. So when their routines are interrupted, when they are thrust into the new and the unknown, they don't always know how to cope with it. This can lead to anxiety and sensory overload among other things.

They Don't See the World as We Do

We've already shown you in previous chapters how neurodivergent people can see things in ways we do not. But what does that really mean in terms of the world we live in? One analogy would be that an autistic person sees the world from the inside of a glass room. Sure, they can see and hear everything that goes on outside, but just like it can with light, sometimes, that glass magnifies some of what comes through—sometimes to the point where it's unbearable. Other times, it can make things murky and less clear. And even though they can see through the glass, they can't just reach out and interact with people on the outside. Because try as they might, that door doesn't open from the inside very easily. Sure, they can force it open for a bit from time to time, but that takes a great amount of effort and energy.

But, if you understand some of their struggles, you can help them force that door open, and maybe a little wider for a little longer. It all depends on how much effort you want to put in to help meet them halfway.

PTSD in Autistic People

Post Traumatic Stress Disorder (PTSD) is when the body's natural fight or flight instincts don't shut down properly. This disorder is the result of a traumatic experience that a person has gone through. Though the experience might have happened days, months, or even years ago, the mind is still affected by the incident, and certain triggers related to the incident can cause the mind to go back into that fight or flight scenario. This can affect them even when they don't feel stressed or frightened, making the disorder difficult to manage if the triggers are not properly understood.

PTSD is typically associated with soldiers who have fought in war, and first responders such as police, fire fighters, and paramedics. Survivors of various traumas, like physical or sexual assault, or those who have survived disasters, can also obtain PTSD from the experience. But autistic people are also prone to experiencing PTSD as well.

Autistic people are more prone to be affected by PTSD than neurotypical people in part because of their condition, but also because of society. Hypersensitivity and the inability at times to process emotions can make it easier for an autistic person to suffer trauma. Changes to routine, extreme sensory experiences (such as a person with hypersensitive hearing hearing a fire alarm), and being prevented from taking part in comforting behaviors such as stimming, are examples of specific traumas that could lead to PTSD.

Some aspects of ASD can also make the onset of PTSD easier, as well as maintaining it for prolonged periods of time. Autistic people with difficulty regulating emotions, as well as those who tend to be highly detailed focus, are suspected to be more inclined towards developing PTSD. Likewise, people with inflexible thinking, or a tendency towards avoidance or increased rumination (the inability to stop thinking about certain things), can also fall prey to PTSD.

Society can also provide its own share of trauma for an autistic person. Things like bullying and abandonment by a loved one can have a more traumatic effect on an autistic person than on a neurotypical person. Difficulties in communicating can also lead to bad experiences that can be traumatic for an autistic person. Others forcing change on an autistic person, or interrupting/breaking routines, can also be traumatic, particularly if they are not expected and there is no support to cope with the resulting fallout.

COMMON PROBLEMS AFFECTING PEOPLE WITH ASD

While we have already mentioned these a few times in the previous chapter, here we will go through some of the common mental health issues people with ASD can experience.

Anxiety

Everyone experiences anxiety at some point. Fear is one of those primal emotions embedded deep in our very beings. Fear can help us survive potentially dangerous situations by warning us of what we might not immediately notice. Even when there is no danger, fear and anxiety can be present when a person is faced with a stressful or challenging situation. It can make us alert, help spur us on, and motivate us to solve problems. But fear can also be just as debilitating and restricting, as anyone who has ever experienced an anxiety disorder can tell you. However, unlike what neurotypical people typically experience, fear and anxiety are things that autistic people can experience on a daily basis just by going about their lives.

As we've already shown, navigating the neurotypical world can be daunting for an autistic person. But even if they seem like they are doing so without too much trouble on the outside, inside might be a different story. Many autistic people, particularly those who have issues with socializing and hypersensitivity. Studies have shown that anxiety is common around 40-50% of autistic people (Anxiety, 2021).

While the causes of anxiety can vary, the symptoms regardless of the source are common, and can include:

- Restlessness, agitation, or distress
- Irregular or increased heartbeat
- Faster breathing or shortness of breath
- Sweating and hot flashes
- Nausea
- Panic attacks

An autistic person may also experience the following symptoms:

- Seeks reassurance more often or constantly
- Avoids certain situations or objects
- Meltdowns, outbursts, and tantrums

- Overthinking and thought paralysis
- Repetitive behavior, such as stimming
- Returning to their normal routines, sometimes obsessing over them
- Running away
- Self-harm

Treating anxiety can be difficult depending on its severity. Counseling, therapy, and medication can help an autistic person deal with their anxiety, and perhaps even build up tolerance to the things that make them anxious. This can include mindfulness training, low arousal techniques to help reduce stress, and exposure therapy, where the autistic person is gradually exposed to the source of anxiety so they can build tolerance to it.

On a more personal level, understanding what triggers the anxiety, and being able to monitor and manage stress levels, can help the autistic person deal with anxiety. Knowing these things can also help you help an autistic person manage their anxiety, much in the same ways as described in chapter 4.

Depression

Depression can be a serious issue for autistic people. Studies have shown that they are four times more likely to experience depression than neurotypical people. This should not be surprising. ASD can be a very crippling disorder, one that comes with many challenges. Difficulties living with ASD, as well as many of the social-related issues, can lead to low self-esteem, anxiety, and (in the long term) depression. This can be accelerated by instances of bullying or failed attempts at socializing.

While the social component can play a large role in autistic people falling prey to depression, it is not the only factor. Scientists and researchers are still unclear what other triggers can bring about depression in autistic people. What we do know is that depression is more likely the higher the IQ of the autistic person. A familial history of depression can also increase the chances of an autistic person becoming depressed, as well as other mental and physical conditions. Children and young adults are more likely to fall prey to depression, while adults are less likely to. However, those who experience depression at a younger age can often carry it with them into adulthood, where it can worsen over-time, particularly if it goes undiagnosed.

Some of the symptoms of depression among autistic people are shared with the neurotypical form of depression, and can include:

- Feelings of hopelessness
- Constant feelings of sadness or low mood
- Always feeling tired
- Lack of energy
- Irregular sleep schedules and patterns
- Neglecting hobbies and interests
- Difficulties at work, or at home with family
- Suicidal thoughts

Some of the symptoms of depression specific to autistic people revolve around some of their regular coping mechanisms that are used more frequently, but with no apparent reason. This can include:

- Obsessive behavior
- Social withdrawal
- Stimming, body rocking, and other unusual physical behaviors
- Aggressive and oppositional behavior
- Self-harm

Unfortunately, because of some traits that can be present in an autistic person, diagnosing them with depression can be difficult. There is little research in ways to effectively screen for depression in autistic people. This can be made further difficult if the autistic person has challenges speaking, as talk therapy is one of the common ways to treat depression. While medication can also be used to treat depression, there is also little research to show whether these medications are effective in treating people with autism, or if they could have other unintended effects.

Despite these potential challenges and unknowns, medication and some forms of therapy, such as mindfulness training and emotional awareness training, have been shown to help autistic people combat their depression.

Task Paralysis

While neurotypical people can be affected by task paralysis, this condition is more common among people with ASD. People with ADHD also tend to experience task paralysis on a regular basis, albeit for different reasons.

Task paralysis is when one is faced with multiple tasks that need to be done, but are overwhelmed by the tasks and the work to be done. This can cause a delay in tasks being done, either preventing them from being done in a timely fashion, or in more severe cases, abandoned altogether to be done at a later date.

Neurotypical people often attribute task paralysis to either being lazy or unmotivated. However, lack of time, resources, or knowledge can also be factors that can contribute to task paralysis. For people with ASD however, it takes on a whole other form, with different triggers and symptoms.

While depression can be a common cause of task paralysis, there are other triggers that can directly relate to an autistic person's traits, and can include:

- Difficulty paying attention or focusing
- Getting or staying organized
- Managing emotions
- Keeping track of current tasks being performed

Anxiety can also be a common factor in task paralysis, particularly if the task is one the autistic person is not familiar with. Learning new things can be daunting for an autistic person, who often relies on what is already known and familiar to them. And because of the way autistic traits can affect even simple daily chores, like washing dishes or folding laundry, it can make task paralysis all the more easy to fall into.

Task paralysis in autistic people can be difficult to manage. Tasks that are avoided can become more daunting, particularly when more tasks get added to the to-do list. This can lead to feelings of anxiety and worry over not completing the task, which could eventually lead to other negative thoughts. In response, many autistic people will shut down, or shift focus to other more familiar tasks to try and avoid the negative thoughts. This however, is only temporary, and after some time of being distracted, the task returns to the forefront of their mind, beginning the cycle anew.

Treating task paralysis can be relatively simple, and generally requires only some forethought. Organization can be key to dealing with task paralysis, as is managing the tasks and the energy required to do them. If the autistic person is feeling overwhelmed by the tasks, try just focusing on one or two tasks, and breaking them down into smaller tasks to help make them more manageable. Adjusting the to-do list might also be necessary, and taking breaks to recover between tasks can also go a long way in helping manage the stress and anxiety that might come from choice paralysis.

Incorporating regular tasks into a routine can also help an autistic person avoid task paralysis. Once something is part of a routine, it can require less thought and energy to perform. If not, the structure of the routine will at least make sure that the task is more likely to get done, as breaking routine would be worse for the autistic person than not doing the task.

Choice Paralysis

Similar to task paralysis, choice paralysis is when an autistic person is faced with a number of options, and can't make a decision on which to pick. The choices can be anything from what to choose on a menu, what color shirt to wear, or which task to start on first.

Choice paralysis is different from task paralysis in that, while task paralysis can be avoided, choice paralysis generally cannot be. Eventually, the autistic person will have to make a choice, but oftentimes this will be when they are at their wits' end. They will choose whatever just to be done with the choice, or try to delegate the task to another person. Choices made in this way are not always the best choices, and are made more to just get them done and over with. Like task paralysis, choice paralysis can cause anxiety, as well as depression, in the long run if the autistic person keeps making poor choices while affected by choice paralysis.

There are ways to avoid choice paralysis. Giving the autistic person time to think about what to choose before having to make the choice can help them sort through the options. For example, if going to a restaurant they haven't been to before, looking up the menu online before going to the restaurant can give them more time to look through it and make a better choice.

TURNING TO THE WRONG THINGS TO COPE

When one thinks of addiction, one tends to think about gambling, drugs and opioids, alcohol, and smoking. But there are many other addictions that are out there. Addictions to pornography, gaming, and even to exercise, are among the few that have been talked about over the years.

Addiction is a trap many people fall into, including autistic people. When faced with difficulty or hardship, we all turn to things that can help us cope and make us feel better. If only for a little while, we want to forget about our daily struggles, and feel like all is right in our world. But sometimes, our quest for peace can come with euphoric feelings that we can easily become addicted to. At the same time, some activities and substances that are used to chase those feelings become addictive in their own way.

While there is no hard evidence that shows autistic people are more likely to succumb to addictions than neurotypical people, recent studies have shown that people struggling with addiction are more likely to have some form of undiagnosed autism. One study done at an outpatient substance-abuse clinic showed that 20% of the people around the eighteen-year age category had higher scores on the Social Responsiveness Scale-2 test (MGH News and Public Affairs, 2022). The Social Responsiveness Scale-2 test is normally done by parents and teachers, and is used to help determine if a child might be autistic.

Another Taiwanese study found that people with autism are at a higher risk of developing a Substance Use Disorder (SUD). The study found that patients with autism were three times more likely to develop a drug use disorder, and a two-fold risk of developing an alcohol use disorder (Monaco, 2021). The risk of SUD was further increased if the patient had certain psychiatric comorbidities, including intellectual disability, ADHD, epilepsy, OCD, mood disorder, anxiety disorder, and impulse control disorder (Monaco, 2021). But while these comorbidities increased the risk of SUD, autistic people as a whole were shown to be at a higher risk than neurotypical people.

It is not hard to imagine people with ASD succumbing more easily to addiction. Compared to neurotypical people, people with ASD face more challenges in daily life, and as a result, more hardship. While most find ways to cope with the stress and anxiety of life that are not destructive, and while they can seem to help in the short term, addictive behavior and substances will do nothing but bring more pain and misery in the long term.

While there are a myriad of things one can become addicted to, the symptoms of addiction can be universal, and can include (Addiction, 2021):

- Increased risky behavior, either physical, mental, or financial
- Regular or excessive use of alcohol, drugs, or other substances
- Lack of control or inability to stop certain activities

Autistic people can also develop addictions due to (Addiction, 2021):

- A lack of help to manage emotions
- A lack of suitable support and services
- A need for routine and repetitiveness
- Co-occurring mental and physical health conditions
- A late diagnosis of autism resulting in a lack of understanding and support

Addiction treatment can be challenging even for neurotypical people. Treating addiction in an autistic person can be even more challenging depending on their autistic traits. Cognitive Behavioural Therapy (CBT) is shown to be particularly effective in treating autistic people with addiction.

Tying It All Together

- Nearly everything in the modern world is designed for the neurotypical, not the neurodivergent
- People with ASD can see the world very differently from the way the neurotypical do
- Many autistic people suffer from Post Traumatic Stress Disorder (PTSD)
- Anxiety and Depression are common issues that autistic people face, often as a result of being unable to easily interact with others and the world around them
- Task paralysis is when an autistic person has difficulty getting tasks, like a daily chores list, done. It is often caused by feeling overwhelmed or by wanting to avoid doing unpleasant tasks

- Choice paralysis is when an autistic person has difficulty making a choice. As with task paralysis, they can be overwhelmed by the amount of choices or information attached to the choices
- Autistic people are more likely to fall victim to addiction as a means of trying to cope with their autistic traits and challenges

6

BLACK AND WHITE THINKING

Mike isn't doing too good. His mom just picked him up from his friend Steve's birthday party. Now that he is safe in his mom's car, Mike breaks down and starts crying. He hates Steve. Steve made him look bad. They've been friends since they were little, but not anymore. Mike doesn't want to see Steve ever again.

Steve is confused as he watches Mike and his mom drive away. It's his tenth birthday today. They were having a good time, and were about to have cake and open presents. But then Donny started to talk about video games. Mike's always been really good at the different games they play, but when Steve corrected Mike about the story for one of them, Donny made

fun of him. Steve did too. He was just joking. But
Mike got angry, real angry. He pushed Steve, and
punched Donny in the face. It was just a game. Why
did he do that?

Inflexibility is a common trait among people with ASD. Most autistic people have an inability to adapt, or difficulty learning new things. Because of this, following routines helps them not only stay in control, but also gives them comfort and a sense of familiarity that can help them cope with their autistic traits. This can also include simple black and white, yes or no type thinking. It's not that the autistic person doesn't want to be more nuanced or diverse in their way of thinking. More often than not, they adopt these ways of thinking because they are limited by their autistic traits, or it is an easier way to help them deal with their autistic traits and challenges.

But how exactly does thinking work? And why are autistic people more prone to black and white thinking than neurotypical people? Part of it has to do with their autistic traits and the challenges that stem from them. This can include deficiencies in the way they think and manage information. In order to better understand this, first we must look at the way people think in general.

COGNITIVE FLEXIBILITY

When we think of being flexible, we often think of gymnastics and acrobatic performers, and the way they can move about as if their joints were elastic. Or yoga, which is another activity that requires a greater than normal amount of flexibility in our muscles and joints. Our brains are no different, in that they can also be flexible.

Cognitive flexibility is the ability for our brain to switch our way of thinking in different ways and perspectives. It allows us to manage and adapt our thinking in various situations. Cognitive flexibility also allows us to multitask by juggling multiple concepts at the same time, as well as to view things at both a micro level of detail and at a macro level. People with good cognitive flexibility are able to more easily handle sudden changes, and are also more able to quickly act appropriately in various situations.

An example of cognitive flexibility would be preparing a meal. During the process, something happens: you might be missing an ingredient, or you might have prepared something wrong. You might find that a piece of equipment you might need, like a blender, is not working. People with high cognitive flexibility can more quickly adapt to the situation by finding an alternative ingredient, or modifying the recipe to suit the current situation. People with lower cognitive flexibility would have a harder time adjusting, and would more likely abandon the recipe or start from scratch.

Cognitive Flexibility and ASD

Autistic people with low cognitive flexibility are viewed as being cognitively inflexible. Consider water in its liquid state. When it flows, water can flow around objects, or over them if there is sufficient buildup. It can also flow under objects if a path becomes available. In this way, water is like cognitive flexibility: It adapts and finds a way forward until it cannot. In this scenario, cognitive inflexibility would be like water that has been frozen: it might be able to move forward, but if it meets an obstacle it is stuck, and will remain stuck until either the obstacle is removed, or the ice is either broken into smaller chunks that can get around the obstacle, or melts completely into water.

People who are cognitively inflexible have a hard time looking at things from different perspectives. They also have trouble adapting to new or sudden situations that might arise. They will also have trouble changing tactics when something does not work like they expect.

For example, if someone who is a vegetarian sits down for a meal with someone who eats meat, they might have a hard time understanding why that person chooses to eat meat. They could have countless correct facts about the benefits of being a vegetarian, and why eating meat is bad, but will not accept the position of others who disagree with them, and will make sure that their stance is known to all at the table.

This form of rigid thinking can be common in people with ASD. The reasoning for it, like many things involving autism, is still not fully understood. However, cognitive inflexibility is not tied to intelligence as some might think. A person can still be highly intelligent, yet still lack the mental flexibility to multitask or adapt to new situations or sudden changes.

While lack of cognitive flexibility isn't always a good or bad thing, an autistic person with too much inflexibility will have difficulty adapting to new environments and situations. It can also impact their ability to interact socially with others. Lack of flexibility is also why some autistic people have a strong preference for routines and predictability in most of what they do: dealing with the known and the predictable fits with cognitive inflexibility, and helps reduce stress and anxiety.

EMOTIONAL FLEXIBILITY

Change is inevitable. Traffic lights change from green to red, sales end and new ones start, and people grow up and move on with their lives, sometimes leaving our sphere of influence, other times coming into it again or for the first time. Because change is inevitable, how we handle that change can tell much about us.

While cognitive flexibility is our ability to switch our thinking based on perspective and situations, emotional flexibility is our ability to manage our emotional responses to situations that might arise. For example, imagine if you had spent a week working on an important project, only to find out after you've completed the work that you made a serious mistake. This mistake will require you to redo a large section of the already completed work. Your first reaction upon realizing the error might be shock at realizing the mistake and its enormity, followed potentially by dismay at the realization, and maybe anger at the thought of having to redo that part of the work. People who have good emotional flexibility will be able to run through these emotions, admit to their mistake, and promptly start working to correct the error, with maybe a little bit of anxiety over the approaching deadline.

Emotional Flexibility and ASD

Among autistic people, emotional flexibility can be difficult to deal with. They can have difficulty managing their emotions due to their autistic traits, and can often swing towards one of two directions. The first is apparent lack of emotion, known as alexithymia. The second, is the inability to manage and regulate emotions, known as emotion dysregulation.

Contrary to what some neurotypical people might think, while some autistic people might come off as being emotionless, they do in fact have emotions. However, some autistic people have trouble identifying their emotions at the moment. For example, if a person is afraid of spiders or other bugs, when they see one, their body would immediately have a fight-or-flight reaction: Your pulse may quicken, your palms might get sweaty, you might gasp, your breathing might quicken, and a burst of adrenaline might be sent through your body. But for people with alexithymia, while their body might have that reaction, their minds will only have a reduced sense of fear, or they might not feel the fear at all. The opposite can also happen, where their mind might feel the fear of seeing a spider, but their body might not react accordingly.

While some autistic people might have issues detecting their emotions, others will have issues controlling them. The opposite of alexithymia is emotion dysregulation, where autistic people have trouble regulating and controlling their emotions. Aside from not always being able to control their emotions in the moment, they can also dwell on negative emotions for hours or even days after the event. For example, an autistic person with emotion dysregulation might have an uncontrolled outburst while meeting a friend, and cause a bit of a scene. The friend reacts negatively to the autistic person, who in turn is hurt by the reaction. The autistic person might dwell on this for days, and become anxious or even depressed until they can move on from the incident. In order to do this, he might require outside intervention in the form of a therapist or other friend to help him get over the incident.

Both alexithymia and emotion dysregulation can have negative effects on an autistic person. In the case of alexithymia, the lack of apparent emotions can be off putting to some people. It can also be a surprise, both to the autistic person and those around them, when they suddenly do show emotion. Lack of emotion can also make it difficult for the autistic person to identify what is wrong with them, particularly when they have a physical reaction, but no (apparent) attached emotional reaction.

For those with emotion dysregulation, it can be a constant struggle to keep their emotions in check. Combined with social challenges, hypersensitivity, and the other challenges associated with their ASD, it can be quite tiring for the autistic person to stay in control. Failure to do so could result in physical or verbal outbursts, or even meltdowns and tantrums.

DISPOSITIONAL FLEXIBILITY

Almost everyone has been told at some point in their lives—and perhaps even at multiple points—to be positive. Negative thoughts breed negative results. Be positive. But there is a little bit more to it than just trying to think happy thoughts all the time.

Our dispositional flexibility is our ability to remain both optimistic and realistic at the same time. It is also the ability to keep calm and level-headed in a situation, staying close to reality while avoiding blind positivity or doomsaying pessimism.

People in leadership positions often have good dispositional flexibility. They are able to remain calm where others might worry or panic. They can make objective decisions in the moment without questioning or second guessing themselves, and can adapt to change as it presents itself without falling prey to any negative emotions that could result from the change. People will look up to them and work with them more readily because they have a steady hand, and are able to give clear and concise orders, while making sure the rest of the team remains calm and cohesive.

A good example of a person with strong dispositional flexibility is a paramedic. Paramedics are found on the scenes of accidents, where those who are present—particularly those who are involved in it or injured—can be emotionally charged. When a paramedic arrives on scene, they must be able to quickly identify and assist those who require aid, and stay calm even during moments where life and death hangs in the balance. They must adapt to sudden changes in their patient's conditions within moments, and must remain on guard in order to ensure their patients arrive at the hospital in the best condition in which they can get them there.

WHAT IS BLACK AND WHITE THINKING?

Cognitive, emotional, and dispositional flexibility are not indicators of intelligence. Rather, they are the indicators of how minds think. As you may have noticed, adaptability is a key word that has been used when talking about all three forms of flexibility. That is because no matter how smart you are either overall, or regarding a specific subject, if you cannot adapt your way of thinking to use that intelligence effectively, it would be no different than not having that intelligence at all. This is a trap many autistic people are caught in: the result being, black and white thinking.

A typical computer CPU (the chip that does all of the information processing) in a computer, at their core, works with data in only one way. While they can carry out complex calculations and processes, the way they manage data is through the use of binary, which is the language of 1s and 0s. Because CPUs and other microchips in general work with electrical signals, there is either an electrical signal, a 1, or no electrical signal, a 0. This combination of ones and zeros are used to represent numbers, which are in turn translated into letters, colors, images, or even sounds. But no matter what the end product is, the CPU still only deals in 1s and 0s.

At its core, black and white thinking is much like how a CPU uses binary to process information. In a CPU, things can only be "true or false", or "on or off". In order to carry out more complex calculations and processes, additional computer programming code—either within the CPU itself, or through programs installed on the computer—must take the output of the CPU, and manipulate it in different ways. For example, if you are watching a movie on your computer, you are likely doing so either through a file (on the computer or being read from a disk like a DVD or blu-ray) or via a stream from the internet. Regardless of the source, the CPU takes the data from the source, processes it, and sends it to the program you are using to watch the video. The program takes the data from the CPU, and turns it into images and sounds that you can see and hear.

What defines black and white thinking is not what it does do, but what it doesn't do. People who think in terms of black and white are like computer CPUs without the support programming to take that data and translate it into things we understand. They can only think in terms of yes or no, or black or white. They either can't see the gray area between those two options, or their thinking is so rigid and set in stone that they can't accept any other option other than true or false.

For example, you are supposed to meet your friend for dinner. You arrive at the restaurant at the appointed time, but your friend is not there. A person with black or white thinking might wait a small amount of time to see if they show up, before deciding that they are not coming, then either leave the place or stay and have dinner without them. A person not fettered by black and white thinking would assume that the friend is still coming, but might be running late, and might try and contact the friend to find out why they are late. But for the black and white thinkers, there are no shades of gray, no third option, and while they won't always assume the worst, they will not hesitate to assume the negative if that is what the evidence supports.

In more extreme cases: Let us say, for example, that you have a particularly bad fight with your friend. Rather than try to calm down and patch things up later, a black and white thinker might just choose to end the friendship based on that one fight. It might seem extreme to the normal person, but for someone who works through black and white thinking, that can be the only logical conclusion. Not because they necessarily want to, but because their rigid, oftentimes inflexible, way of thinking compels them to.

Because of this way of thinking, black and white thinkers tend to try to avoid conflict whenever possible. But avoiding conflict can come with its own problems. The black and white thinker might keep people at a distance, or agree with them even when they internally disagree, in order to avoid conflict. Conflict avoidance can also be done by simply ignoring the problem, though this is often only a short term solution that can lead to a much larger conflict in the future. Avoiding conflict can also build resentment towards the source of the conflict, as well as affect one's own self-esteem.

Cognitive Distortions and How They Affect Thinking

Black and white thinking is considered to be a cognitive distortion. Cognitive distortions are negative or irrational biases, or ways of thinking. They can affect how we see the world and interact with it. They can also affect our mental health by inserting negativity into a situation when there isn't any, or magnifying it when there is little.

People with ASD are more prone to cognitive distortions, but not just because of often-heavy use of black and white thinking. Their autistic traits, and the challenges these can impose upon them, can also lead to the development of cognitive distortions. Most cognitive distortions are formed subconsciously, as a result of lived experience or what we are taught. Because of that, it can be difficult for an autistic person to identify their cognitive distortions, as they seem to be a natural part of their thought process, even when they are unhelpful or a hindrance.

Aside from black and white thinking, there are other cognitive distortions that can affect how an autistic person interacts with others and society as a whole. Here are a few common ones to watch out for.

Emotional Reasoning is when we use emotions to make judgments and decisions. This is not necessarily a bad thing, as many people "listen to their gut" when making decisions. However, for an autistic person this can be problematic, particularly when they are affected by either alexithymia or emotion dysregulation. This can also be made worse by black and white thinking, as an autistic person can easily slide into more negative conclusions. Anxiety can also play a role in bad emotional reasoning, as fear can cause us to err on the side of caution in ways we would not normally consider.

Jumping to conclusions is something we all do from time to time. As neurotypical people, we might jump to a conclusion because we think we already have enough information to predict the outcome of something. While we might not always be right, most of the time, incorrect conclusions do not tend to have great consequences. Guessing the ending of a story wrong, for example, might catch us by surprise, but doesn't otherwise affect us. This is not always the case for autistic people.

Jumping to conclusions can be a symptom of other underlying conditions or cognitive distortions in autistic people. These conclusions are also often rooted in negative thinking, and can be the result of black and white thinking.

Magnification or minimizing essentially prioritizes the wrong things in life. Often focusing on negative things, the magnification distortion makes these things out to be bigger issues than they really are. Minimizing does the opposite, lessening the impact of oftentimes positive accomplishments and achievements. This can create a skewed perception where things are worse than they might actually appear. Magnification and minimization are often common in people who suffer from panic attacks.

Personalization occurs when the person blames themselves when things go wrong, even when they were not at fault. This happens when a person thinks they have more control over a situation than they actually do. Because of this, they see any negative result as being their fault for occurring, even when there is no conceivable way that they could have been responsible.

For example, you make reservations at a restaurant where your friend has a favorite dish. But when they go to order, that favorite dish is not currently available. This could be because the kitchen is out of a key ingredient, or a piece of equipment (like a specialized oven) is currently not working. Perhaps a food order was not placed or did not arrive in time, or maybe that dish was just more popular than usual that day. But regardless of the reason, you feel responsible for ruining your friend's evening because they couldn't order that one dish.

CHALLENGING BLACK AND WHITE THINKING

Unlike other autistic traits, black and white thinking is not something that is a part of an autistic person. Rather, it is a way of thinking that was developed over time either as a result of trying to cope with their autistic traits, or by other experienced trauma or negative life experiences. Just as black and white thinking can be learned, it can also be unlearned, with time and patience. However, for some autistic people with more pronounced autistic traits, black and white thinking can also be a mechanism which they rely on to help make it through daily life. Trying to get rid of black and white thinking, particularly if the autistic person is not ready to do so, can be damaging.

While dealing with black and white thinking should primarily be left to a therapist, there are things you can do to help an autistic person. While they might not be able to overcome black and white thinking altogether, they can help in a given situation.

The first thing you can do to make a difference is to **avoid using black and white words**. Black and white thinking deals with absolutes: A or B, and nothing before, after, or in between. To help get out of that mind set, avoid using words that are more lofty, or concrete. This can include words like, "always", "impossible", "perfect", "disaster", "ruined", to name a few. Instead, try using more gray area language, and words that are more open to interpretation. This can include words like "sometimes", "noticing", "willing", "prefer", "flexible", etc. For example, instead of saying "I can't go at that time", use "I'd prefer to go at this time".

When confronted with black and white thinking, **ask for proof**. Most cognitive distortions are based on negative views and thoughts. They may sound reasonable at first, but if put under scrutiny, they are often shown to be flawed thinking. By forcing the autistic person to think about whether something is true or not, by proving its validity or lack thereof, can help them come to realize that the statement is indeed false, and shouldn't be so readily believed.

Black and white thinking can often cloud judgment. Sometimes, all an autistic person needs is to **get clarification**. If they are struggling with a decision, it might be because they lack the necessary information to make a proper decision. If you think an autistic person is struggling with a question, ask them if there is something they need clarified.

Mindfulness is a skill that helps an autistic person overcome black and white thinking. This is the practice of being able to look at one's own thoughts and actions without judgment. This can be done through exercises like guided meditation, or five sense exercises. Practicing mindfulness can help an autistic person become aware of their black and white thinking, making it easier to overcome in the long term.

Black and white thinking can also come from being hyper-focused on a subject or issue. Because of this, an autistic person might overlook some other options. In some cases, **making a list of other possibilities** can help them overcome black and white thinking in given situations by forcing them to think about alternatives that might not otherwise fit into their black and white thinking. Making a list can also help combat negative thinking when it is present, as it can force the autistic person to consider other possibilities that might be opposite of the negative thought.

Tying It All Together

- The way we think can be broken up into three types of "flexibility": cognitive, emotional, and dispositional
- Cognitive flexibility is our ability to switch our way of thinking and multitask by juggling multiple concepts in our mind
- Some autistic people have cognitive inflexibility
- Emotional flexibility is our ability to manage our emotional responses
- Some autistic people can have either alexithymia, which is the inability to detect our own emotions, or emotion dysregulation, the inability to control or contain emotions
- Dispositional flexibility is our ability to keep our thoughts grounded, by being neither too optimistic or pessimistic
- Black and white thinking is a cognitive distortion where thinking is excessively rigid
- Other cognitive distortions that can accompany black and white thinking include emotional reasoning, jumping to conclusions, personalization, and magnification or minimizing

- You can help an autistic person avoid black and white thinking by doing things like avoiding the use of black and white words, asking for proof when they make black and white statements or conclusions, or helping them get clarification on a subject
- An autistic person can avoid black and white thinking by practicing techniques to help them be more cognitively flexible

7

THE PROBLEM WITH EXECUTIVE FUNCTION

Fred has an eye for details. His hobby is modeling and painting miniatures. Planes, trains, game pieces, anything that can be put together and painted, and requires an eye for details, is his bread and butter. His eye for detail has also helped him in his job as an accountant. Sure, the numbers are a little harder to understand sometimes, but once he figures them out, he can find every last little detail that needs to be found.

Unfortunately, Fred can get a little too caught up in his hunt for details. He can get so focused on a spreadsheet that he loses track of time, and his work suffers for it. His focus on detail has also been the butt of many jokes around the office—something made worse by the fact that Fred is more than a little awkward around others. Still, for all his "failing", he tries his best to make it through the day. He just wishes sometimes that work didn't take so much out of him.

In the last chapter, we talked about how we think and showed you how ASD can affect the way autistic people can think. However, thinking is just one of a number of cognitive functions that a person needs in order to live their lives. The functions and the skills related to them are known as executive functions.

WHAT IS EXECUTIVE FUNCTION?

Executive function is perhaps best described as the management system of the brain. It consists of three critical functions: cognitive flexibility, the working memory, and inhibitory control, also known as self-control. A person's executive function is tied to many skills we use in our daily lives, including:

- Organizing, planning, and prioritizing
- Paying attention
- Problem solving
- Starting tasks, and staying focused on that task, until completion

- Reasoning
- Regulating emotions and inhibiting inappropriate responses
- Self-monitoring (such as keeping track of what you are currently doing)
- Understanding different points of view

Executive function plays a role in many of the tasks we do daily. Planning a weekend getaway, organizing a work event, preparing a meal, doing laundry, putting a puzzle together. All of these things require some part of executive function in order to do properly and correctly.

Just by looking at the above list, you probably recognize some of things that autistic people can have issues with. A few of these we have discussed in some way in previous chapters. That is because many people with ASD have challenges when it comes to their executive functions. However, executive function challenges can be a little more difficult to spot, as some of the challenges an autistic person can face are similar to signs of ADHD. Because ADHD primarily affects a person's executive function, autistic people with executive function challenges can often be mistaken for having ADHD. Some of the challenges autistic people have with their executive function can include:

- Trouble starting and/or completing tasks
- Difficulty prioritizing tasks
- Forgetting what they just read or heard
- Trouble following directions or a sequence of steps
- Panic when rules or routines change
- Trouble switching from one task to another
- Get overly emotional
- Become fixated on specific objects or topics
- Difficulty organizing their thoughts
- Have trouble keeping track of their belongings
- Find it difficult to manage their time

Looking at this list, you might notice a few points that you might be guilty of from time to time. This does not mean you have issues with executive function. People with executive functions will have challenges in one or several of these areas on a daily basis, sometimes to the point where it can affect their ability to get work done. A person with executive function challenges, for example, might be able to focus on tasks and complete them quickly, but might need far more time to prepare for the task, or to start the task after switching to another one. A person might get so engrossed in a subject or task, that they might lose focus on all else that goes on around them, including the passing of time.

While executive function challenges are common among people with ASD, they are not the only group that can experience executive function challenges. As we already mentioned, ADHD also primarily affects executive function. But the cause of both executive function challenges and ADHD are still a mystery.

In many cases, executive function challenges are the result of neurodivergent brain growth. However, ADHD is often seen as being hereditary, with the parent passing it on to the child. While there is a higher chance of giving birth to a child with ASD if it is present in the family tree, it is not guaranteed to be passed on from parent to child with the same frequency as ADHD. People with learning disabilities like dyslexia or dyscalculia can also experience executive function challenges, though not always.

EARTH TO...

For various reasons, focusing can be a difficult thing for autistic people to do. Hypersensitivity, and the inability to filter out extraneous sensory input, can affect an autistic person's ability to focus. This can in turn affect their attention span.

Types of Attention

Our attention span is our ability to focus on a specific task for extended periods of time. However, what that means exactly can vary. Researchers across many disciplines often differ in their theories, methodologies, and even terminology when it comes to attention span. However, over time, a number of common definitions have been formed.

Sustained attention is one of the two generally accepted definitions of attention. This is our ability to focus on a specific task or stimuli for an extended period of time without being distracted. Watching a movie, reading a book, or playing a video game are examples of sustained attention.

Selective attention is the second of the two generally accepted definitions of attention. Selected attention is our ability to focus on a single task or stimuli while being surrounded by others. It is our ability to filter out distracting stimuli, and focus on the one we are interested in. Listening to announcements in a busy store or mall, reading or watching a video on a crowded bus, or focusing on one person's voice while sitting in a crowd, are examples of selective attention.

There are also a few other forms of attention that are also widely accepted, and are important in both clinical settings and in daily life.

Alternating attention is our ability to shift focus from one task to another. A common example of this would be reading an instruction, and then carrying out that instruction. It can also include things like writing down information after reading it, or even things such as talking, and then stopping to eat or take a drink.

Divided attention is often confused with multitasking, something that the human mind cannot really do. Divided attention is our ability to focus on two or more tasks at once. But while we may claim we are good at multitasking, what we are really doing is just focusing on parts of both tasks, not on both tasks as a whole. Because we are not giving either task our full attention, they are not being done as fast or as properly as they could be. Talking on a cell phone while driving is a good example of this.

The Challenge of Attention With ASD

Back in chapter 2, we talked about camouflage and how it can be both physically and mentally draining for the autistic person. But even an autistic person who isn't trying to camouflage can still experience cognitive fatigue (also known as mental fatigue) just by being who they are.

In America, a neurotypical person is expected to put in a full day's work, and then either go home or go out to enjoy their hobbies. While most neurotypical people might be able to do this during an average day, it can be a different story for the neurodivergent. Autistic people who have trouble with focusing, or other difficulties related to attention, have to expend far more energy in order to do the same daily tasks that the neurotypical do. But the amount of energy they need to put into it can vary. Depending on their autistic traits, one autistic person might need to spend more energy on a single task than another. For example, a person with Asperger's syndrome may have an easier time doing laundry than a person with more common ASD symptoms. But when it comes to socializing with others, both might have to spend the same amount of energy on paying attention to the task of socializing.

Depending on their traits and challenges, autistic people are more likely to experience mental fatigue faster than a neurotypical person. This can not only affect their mental state, but also their performance. As their mental fatigue increases, sustained attention decreases. It becomes harder to stay focused on tasks. While this is also true for neurotypical people, it is more serious for autistic people because it also becomes more difficult to manage their autistic traits.

In order for autistic people to excel, they need to be able to focus. This mainly involves removing as many distractions as possible. Creating a sensor-friendly environment, for example, can help an autistic person focus by eliminating potential distractions. Many of the other tips described in chapter 4 can also be used to help an autistic person's attention span, as eliminating unwanted stimuli removes most of the potential distractions that could prevent them from concentrating.

Hyperfocus and Hyperfixation

Often used interchangeably—and incorrectly—hyperfocus and hyperfixation are symptoms of both ASD and ADHD.

Hyperfocus is the ability to focus deep and overt concentration on a subject or task for long periods of time. This can be beneficial, as it allows a person to focus and learn about a subject to the point where they can be deemed unique and gifted. However, being hyperfocused can also be detrimental, because tasks and traits that are not the subject of the focus, or associated with it, can suffer to the point where it can affect an autistic person's quality of life.

Hyperfixation is an extreme fixation on a subject, be it a show, hobby, a certain type of cloth, or even a person or thought. When someone becomes hyperfixated on something, they want to know anything and everything about the subject. Neurotypical people might call this an obsession, but for an autistic person, it can become a coping mechanism to deal with stress. And unlike hyperfocus, which will only last until the autistic person loses interest or shifts their focus to something else, hyperfixation can last for years.

Treating either hyperfocusing or hyperfixation, or both, can be done in the same way. Aside from CBT, keeping a schedule or timetable and adhering to it can help treat either condition. Also, keeping a disciplined environment around the subject of focus or fixation can also help to limit exposure. Some medications can also help dull the effect of both conditions, though in order to fully get either condition under control, working with a therapist is the optimal solution.

ACTING ON IMPULSE

Acting on impulse is a very human thing. We've all done it, probably more times than we might be able to count, or are willing to admit. Everyone does it: men, women, children, teenagers, adults. At some point, something will catch our eye, an idea will pop into our head, or an opportunity will present itself, and without thinking, we will act upon it. Now, whether that ends up being a good idea or not, that is another story.

Impulsivity is defined as making decisions based on emotions or the spur of the moment. Impulsivity is a double-edged sword: Taking chances or "following your gut" can result in benefits. But at the same time, it can also get you into trouble. People who are described as being hot-headed, rash, unpredictable, and unstable, have low impulse control, and they often get in trouble for it. For the neurotypical, acting on impulse can be a fine line between being smart and lucky, or stupid and brash depending on the results. Impulse control for autistic people is a little more complicated. Because many autistic people have executive function challenges, this can affect their ability to manage and suppress their impulses.

When people think of those with ASD, they often think of the way autistic people do stimming, or other strange behaviors. Many attribute this to acting out or, "that's just what autistic people do". But as we've shown, there are very real reasons why autistic people, and to some extent, neurodivergent people in general, do what they do. In the case of people with ASD, lack of impulse control is far more serious because it doesn't just stop at making questionable decisions. Autistic people with impulse control issues have difficulty controlling their wants and needs.

When they want something, like a specific item, they want it now and will not wait patiently. If they are hungry, they want to eat now, regardless of what might be going on around them. If they are bored with the current task, they will abandon it in favor of something else, potentially disrupting others around them.

Lack of impulse control can also extend into emotional control. This results in a limited ability in controlling one or more of their emotions. Rather than control or internalize their emotions, an autistic person with impulse control issues is more likely to get angry, start to cry, or yell. It can also lead to hyperfocusing and hyperfixation, as the autistic person will lack the ability to suppress their desires and interests.

Impulse control issues can be the most taxing of autistic traits for caregivers. Not only do autistic people with this issue have to be monitored more closely, but their lack of impulse control can also be dangerous. For example, if an autistic person has a strong interest in cars, and they see cars driving by on a busy road, their impulse might be to go get a better look, potentially causing them to wander into traffic. Or if, say, their attention is caught by a specific color, they may want to go examine any object of the same color, even if that object is dangerous.

TIME MANAGEMENT ISSUES

Time management can be another challenge for autistic people in their day to day lives. Neurotypical people can often lose track of time, or not properly manage their time when working on various tasks. This is usually due to either poor planning or overestimation.

While poor time management skills can be due to executive function challenges, there is a little more nuance to it for autistic people. Studies have found that people with ASD have difficulties perceiving time in the same ways that neurotypical people do. This not only includes keeping track of time, but also gauging how much time has gone by, as well as understanding the 'concept' of time and the language surrounding it. However, the results of these studies have produced conflicting results with one another.

One study done in 2010 found that adults with autism had difficulties gauging the duration of sounds (Mascarelli, 2010). In this particular study, researchers found that the autistic adults were overestimating the duration of short tones, while overestimating the duration of long tones. The responses of the autistic adults were also far broader than those of the neurotypical control group, which tended to be much more consistent.

A similar study done in 2012 with autistic children tended to show the opposite (Gil et al, 2012). Twenty-four children—twelve autistic, twelve not—otherwise identical in age, sex, chronological, and mental age, were exposed to tones of different ranges. The result of the experiment showed that the children with ASD had the same reaction time as the neurotypical children.

Other experiments done over the last decade have also come up with mixed results. A recent systematic review, done by the Wiley Online Library, of various timing and time perception experiments made some interesting findings. One of their biggest findings is that despite the research that has been done so far, there are still many unanswered questions. However, they also acknowledge that autistic people have the same internal clock that neurotypical people do, yet due to various cognitive impairments, they can have trouble perceiving and interpreting time the same way neurotypical people do. The why of it though, requires further study.

An autistic person's ability to perceive and manage time can be impaired based on their autistic traits and challenges. If an autistic person has issues with memory, it can affect how they perceive time. Some cognitive impairments, like hyperfocusing, can also affect how an autistic person tracks time. An inability to track time can also affect an autistic person's social skills.

Helping an autistic person manage their time better can be tricky depending on their issues with time management. If they have trouble with just managing their time, creating a schedule or a to-do list for the day can be beneficial. However, try not to be too focused on micromanaging time. This can be stressful for an autistic person, and can also create anxiety or lower self-esteem when they fail to start or finish a task on time.

If an autistic person has trouble perceiving time, visual aids can be helpful. For example, a traditional twelve-hour analog clock, while difficult for some neurotypical people to read, can be even more difficult for an autistic person to understand. A digital clock is much simpler to read. Things like timers and sand hourglasses can also be used to help more 'visually' demonstrate the passage of time.

Visual Scheduling

While structure and routine can greatly help an autistic person make it through the day, these are not enough on their own to help them manage time effectively. Just because an autistic person does tasks A, B, and C, in a specific order all the time, does not mean that all three will be done in the same amount of time every time. When an autistic person has issues with time management, they will need extra support and motivation to help them better keep track of time. While schedules and planners can be helpful in this regard, if an autistic person has trouble reading, a visual schedule can be more effective.

A visual schedule is similar to a normal schedule or day planner, but rather than focus on time, it focuses on the tasks and goals to be completed. Visual schedules also use color or images to show specific tasks, making them stand out more than just by writing them down. Some schedules use removable pieces so that a task can be removed from the schedule to show completion, or just a simple checkbox. Being able to mark a task as completed in some way, not only shows that the task is done, but can also be very satisfying and uplifting for an autistic individual.

Planning a visual schedule for an autistic person can be fairly straightforward. The first step is to break the day and/or week into more manageable chunks. For example, a day can be broken into morning, afternoon, and evening, or into smaller chunks of two to four hours a piece. The idea is to avoid assigning tasks based on specific hourly times. If an autistic person misses doing an assigned task at a specific time, it can feel like a failure to them, even if they manage to complete the task successfully.

Once the time frame has been sufficiently broken up, the next step is to determine what goals are to be accomplished during that time frame. For example, a goal could be, reading three times a week, or cleaning twice a week. When determining the goals, don't try to be overly specific. For example 'what to clean and when' is better off in a cleaning to-do list, and should not be added to the schedule. Avoid trying to be too detailed in the visual schedule to avoid confusion and/or stress.

Once goals have been determined, they can be added to the schedule. Going back to the previous example, if you want to clean twice a week, you would devote two chunks of time to cleaning. When filling out the schedule, make sure there are sufficient breaks and downtime between goals. This can help an autistic person recover between tasks, and prevents stress from building up. Also make sure not to over-commit when scheduling, and to not leave a time sensitive task to the last minute.

Visual schedules can be made by hand, but there are also apps and programs that can be used on various devices. While not all of the available apps are designed for autistic people, they can be adapted for use by following the process mentioned above.

Tying It All Together

- Executive function is a combination of cognitive flexibility, memory, and self-control
- Executive function challenges are not limited to autism. People with ADHD also have similar challenges
- There are two types of attention: sustained attention, our ability to focus on a single thing for an extended period, and selective attention, our ability to do this whilst excluding everything else
- Alternative attention is our ability to shift our focus from one thing to another

- Divided attention is our ability to keep our attention on parts of multiple things at the same time
- Humans do not have the ability to truly multitask, i.e., focus completely on two or more things at the same time
- Autistic people often need to use more energy to focus on things than neurotypical people
- Hyperfocusing is the ability to focus deeply and intently on a single thing or subject
- Hyperfixation is when an autistic person becomes fixated on a subject or topic
- Autistic people have trouble managing time partially because they either have issues perceiving time, or trouble understanding time
- Schedules and routines can help an autistic person manage their time, while aids like digital clocks, timers, and sand hourglasses can help them perceive time
- A visual schedule can convert this information into an easy-to-understand format

8

MAYBE... GETTING A DIAGNOSIS

Diane always knew she was different. She's always had trouble fitting in and socializing with others. She has a very logical mind, and is great at solving puzzles and other problems, as long as they're interesting. If they're not, then good luck getting Diane to even look at them.

Over the years, Diane learned little tricks and ways to help her cope with socializing. But that didn't stop it from being hard, exhausting, and almost not worth the effort. But she has a wonderful partner who supports her, and helps her through the tough times.

Then one day, Diane's partner comes to her about a segment they saw in the news about autism. It got

them thinking about Diane and some of her quirks.
The story had left an impression on Diane as well. It
made her think about her life, and its highs and lows.
It made her wonder, if maybe she could be autistic...

M ost cases of autism are diagnosed in children during their early years of development. As we have shown, ASD is the type of disorder that can be very hard to miss when one has pronounced autistic traits. However, we've also shown that while many are diagnosed at an early age, many more are diagnosed much later in life. Women in particular have been historically under diagnosed in terms of autism. But if a person (man or woman) has mild autistic symptoms, such as mild Asperger's syndrome, they can go undiagnosed for a large portion of their life.

GETTING DIAGNOSED

Because of the countless combinations of, and severity of, autistic symptoms and traits, diagnosing someone with autism is not a simple process. Though some autistic symptoms and traits can be very prevalent, they could also be signs of other mental disorders. Because of this, in order to get a proper ASD diagnosis, it must be done by a health professional.

Step 1: Self-Evaluation

If you think you might have autism, the first step might be to take a self-evaluation test. There are several self-evaluation tests that you can take to give you an idea of whether you might be on the spectrum. One such test, the Autism Spectrum Quotient, can be found here. While such self-evaluating tests can be used to give you an idea of what autistic traits you might have, they are not, and should not be taken as, an actual diagnosis.

Step 2: Professional Evaluation

If your self-evaluation tests indicate that you might have some form of autism, the next step is to be evaluated by a medical practitioner. However, not every doctor has the skills and knowledge necessary to diagnose autism. More so, you can't just rely on any doctor with experience of ASD. The processes of diagnosing children and adults are very different. What works for one person, will not work for others. Unfortunately, there are only a small number of clinicians who specialize in diagnosing autism in adults. If you cannot find one, speaking with developmental pediatricians, child specialists, or a pediatric neurologist who specializes in autism, could be a good substitute, but only if they are comfortable with evaluating an adult.

If you are unsure how to find one, try speaking to your family doctor or insurance provider. There are also a number of autism organizations that could provide you information on local doctors that deal with ASD. You can also try various online medical directories that can be searched. However you find that professional, just make sure that they do have experience dealing with autism.

Once you find a professional to evaluate you, they will spend some time over several sessions observing and evaluating you. They may also have to take one or more tests designed for diagnosing autism in adults. Some of the tests they might use could include:

- Autism Diagnostic Observation Schedule, Second Edition (ADOS-2) Module 4
- Developmental, Dimensional, and Diagnostic Interview-Adult Version (3Di-Adult)
- Social Responsiveness Scale (SRS)
- Autism Diagnostic interview-Revised (ADI-R)

If you should be tempted to look into these tests before your evaluation, it is recommended that you do not. These are not the sorts of tests you want to cheat on, either to get, or avoid getting, an ASD diagnosis. These tests, if you take them, are only a part of the overall evaluation, and incorrect information can lead to either a diagnosis taking longer, or some form of misdiagnosis. Also, going through the tests yourself might create unintended bias towards some results. Just because you might think you have a certain autistic trait, does not mean you actually have it. Leave the evaluation and diagnosis to the professionals.

Step 3: Differential Diagnosis and Getting Treatment

The reason why it is so important to be evaluated and diagnosed by a professional is because there are other mental disorders that share similar symptoms with ASD. Some disorders, while they may share similar symptoms as ASD (such as bipolar disorder and some impulse control disorders) are not related to ASD in any way. Others, like ADHD, can also be found in people with ASD, but can also be found on its own in others. This is why other developmental and psychiatric disorders must be ruled out before an autism diagnosis can be made. This can include:

- ADHD
- Anxiety Disorder
- Some form of disruptive, impulse-control, or conduct disorder
- Depression
- OCD

- Bipolar disorder
- Schizophrenia disorder

Once you have received an autism diagnosis, you can begin to look at treatment. Because ASD can be misdiagnosed, and also because ASD can come with other underlying conditions, any medication currently being taken will have to be re-evaluated and adjusted. New medications may also be prescribed. Aside from medication, therapy is also commonly prescribed for adults with ASD. While CBT can be helpful for people with autism, it is not always necessary for adults with mild autistic traits. Any therapy or treatments to be taken or undergone should always be discussed with your therapist or doctor before starting, both to make sure that they will have a beneficial effect, and to make sure they will not complicate any other medical conditions or issues you might have.

Other Conditions That May Come Up During the Diagnosis Process

As we've already shown, autism can look like many things. However, aside from being a spectrum disorder, autism can also come with other disorders as well. Not everyone who is diagnosed with ADHD will have other underlying conditions as well. They can include:

- **Anxiety and Depression:** As we have already shown, both anxiety and depression are common conditions autistic people face. Anxiety can also be a symptom of various phobias, as well as PTSD. Depression can result from a variety of sources, including traumatic events such as an accident or the loss of a loved one. Low mood, sadness, and suicidal thoughts are common symptoms of depression.
- **Attention Deficit Hyperactivity Disorder (ADHD):** ADHD is a disorder characterized by low impulse control, difficulties concentrating, and finding it hard to sit still. Hyperactivity is also a defining trait of ADHD, one that has caused children in the past to be misdiagnosed with ADHD.
- **Dyslexia and Dyspraxia:** Dyslexia is a common disorder where a person has difficulty with either reading, writing, and spelling, or any combination of the three. The severity of dyslexia can range from trouble reading, to difficulty understanding written materials and struggling with planning and organizing. Dyspraxia, also known as Developmental Coordination Disorder (DCD), can affect coordination and fine motor skills. It can have a larger impact on how a person learns skills that

require physical movement, and can also affect how a person interacts with their emotions and social skills. While they can make learning more difficult, both dyslexia and dyspraxia are not considered learning disabilities because they are not affected by a person's intelligence.

- **Epilepsy:** A condition that can cause a person to experience seizures, epilepsy is the result of bursts of electrical activity within the brain that disrupts its normal function. Symptoms of seizures can include collapsing, fits of uncontrollable jerking and shaking, becoming stiff, losing awareness, strange sensations in your limbs, and strange smells and tastes. People who experience epileptic seizures are also known to pass out during the seizure.

- **Insomnia:** Insomnia is a condition where people find it hard to sleep at night. This can include being unable to winding down, waking up multiple times during the night, and waking up and not falling back to sleep. Increased anxiety, as well as hypersensitivity, can also cause insomnia.

- **Learning Disabilities:** While learning disabilities are often associated with low intelligence, having a learning disability does not automatically mean you have low intelligence. Learning disabilities include difficulty understanding complicated information, trouble learning some skills, or looking after oneself. Depending on the type and severity of the disability, a person can still live a relatively normal life despite having a learning disability.

- **Obsessive Compulsive Disorder (OCD):** OCD is when a person has obsessive thoughts that are intrusive and difficult to control. Many deal with these thoughts and other unpleasant feelings by doing repetitive physical or mental behaviors that provide temporary relief. While similar to stimming, stimming by itself is not a trait of OCD.

- **Pain in joints and other body parts:** Some people with ASD also experience some physical effects like flexible or painful joints, skin that can stretch and bruise easily, or persistent diarrhea or constipation. These can also be symptoms of other syndromes, such as joint hypermobility and Ehlers-Danlos.

AVAILABLE TREATMENTS AND SUPPORTIVE EQUIPMENT

Much like how there is no one universal test for diagnosing ASD, there is also not one universal treatment or therapy. Depending on your autistic traits, you might need a little therapy and support, or you might find yourself benefiting from more or even daily support. Therapy can help you overcome or manage a number of your autistic traits. There are also a number of assistive technologies that can help overcome some of the challenges that you might face with ASD.

Before investing in either treatments or supportive equipment, make sure that these are things you need. If you are uncertain about what treatments you might need, consult your doctor or health care provider.

- **Mental Health Therapy:** Perhaps the most common form of support needed by autistic people, mental health therapy can cover a wide array of topics. People see therapists to help deal with other disorders such as anxiety and depression, or to help better manage their autistic traits. They can also help identify and change negative behaviors, as well as help an autistic person manage social interactions by offering strategies or scripts that they can memorize. Different therapists have different tools based on their areas of expertise. Make sure the therapist you see is equipped to deal with your challenges.

- **Occupational Therapy:** Rather than focus on mental health, occupational therapy focuses on learning, retaining, or regaining skills used in daily life or in the workplace. This can include complex skills like using a computer, or simple tasks like eating and drinking, or maintaining balance and coordination. Occupational therapists can also make recommendations in adjusting environments to make them more sensory-friendly to the autistic person. Like mental health therapists, occupational therapists have different areas of expertise. Make sure you find the right therapist to fit your needs and challenges.

- **Speech and Language Therapy:** Speech can be an important way to communicate, even for autistic people. But speech does not just include words and properly formed sentences. It also requires the ability to make the proper sounds and inflections, the quality of the voice, and fluency. Language is also a skill that can be taken for granted by the neurotypical. The ability to express and understand ideas, wants, needs, and feelings is also important. A speech-language pathologist (SLP) can not only help an autistic person learn, relearn, or maintain speech and language, but also help them understand the pragmatics of a language and local dialect as well.

- **Assistive technology for communications (AAC):** Depending on your disability, there are a number of tools and technologies that can help an autistic person better adapt to their challenges. Alternative and Augmentative Communication (AAC) is the practice of using alternative forms of communication. This can include things like drawing, using cue cards, writing, pointing to photos and objects, or even sign language. There are also many devices, both high tech and low tech, that can also be used to speak, or read writing out loud. Many devices, like personal computers, laptops, tablets, and smartphones, also have AAC apps and programs that can be installed to help an autistic person communicate better.

- **Service Animals:** You may have seen blind people with service dogs in the past. They help their owner navigate the world, and can be trained to stop at lights and stop signs, as well as to avoid certain hazards. Autistic people can also benefit from a service animal, and they have been shown to help people with ASD live more independent lives. Aside from navigation, service animals can also be trained to help an autistic person with other tasks, such as preparing for work, alert their owner to the presence of familiar people, and help manage sensory and motor behaviors.

While there are many different types of service animals, including cats, birds, monkeys and even horses, most jurisdictions will not recognize these animals as being service animals. In many cases, dogs are the only recognized service animals permitted into many businesses and establishments. If you do decide to get a service animal of your own, make sure to first acquaint yourself with the local rules and laws regarding service animals, and specifically your preferred type of animal.

DEALING WITH EMOTIONS AFTER A DIAGNOSIS

An ASD diagnosis, particularly one that comes later in life, can be an overwhelming experience. Even if you suspect already that you might have some form of autism, actually receiving that diagnosis can still be a shock, particularly if the autistic symptoms that are identified are not what you are expecting. The shock can be even greater if you are not expecting an ASD diagnosis.

Even if your autistic traits are just mild, an autism diagnosis is life-changing. Things will never be the same for you. Because of this, a diagnosis can come with a mixed bag of emotions. Whether you are diagnosed yourself, or you are a parent whose child has been diagnosed with ASD, you can still experience some of the same emotions. While you might not experience all these emotions, there are four that tend to be common.

Denial is often the first reaction. If we are not ready to face the truth, we will try to deny its existence, that the results are wrong, that the doctor made a mistake. Feelings of denial can be particularly strong if an ASD diagnosis was not one of the expected outcomes. Even when it is, it can be a tough pill to swallow at first. But while denial can help you cope, too much can be detrimental, as the sooner you can accept your autism diagnosis, the sooner you can move on to getting treatment.

After denial comes grief and anger. The two are often linked, and will not always be in equal doses. For parents of a now autistic child, the grief can be particularly strong among parents of autistic children. Why did this happen to my child? What will happen to my child? The death of a future dream can be difficult to let go of, and is often accompanied by anger, blaming others, and jealousy.

Adults who receive a diagnosis of ASD can feel more anger than grief at times. While they might mourn the potential of earlier years lost to the struggles of undiagnosed autism, anger can also be more prevalent. Why didn't someone catch this sooner? Why didn't anyone notice something was wrong? Why didn't anyone listen to me? How would my life have been different, if I had known this sooner? Anger can often be directed at close family members and caregivers, but friends and others can also have anger directed at them.

Acceptance can be a difficult thing to attain for people diagnosed with ASD. After denial, anger, and grief have run their course, acceptance usually comes at the end. But acceptance doesn't always mean peace. Even if a person accepts an ASD diagnosis, they might still harbor feelings of denial, grief, or anger. This can lead to resentment, jealousy, and other more serious problems like anxiety and depression. It can also lead to a person seeking out alternative treatments for autism in the hopes of making it disappear. To truly accept your diagnosis, is to be at peace with the fact that you or your child or loved one is now autistic. Nothing you can say or do will change. All that's left is to keep moving forward, and try to make things better for yourself, and those around you.

TALKING TO OTHERS ABOUT YOUR DIAGNOSIS

Life-changing events rarely go unnoticed. As the name implies, these events can come with significant change in a person's lifestyle and daily habits. These sorts of changes rarely go unnoticed. Even strangers who are accustomed to seeing certain people, will notice when they change the patterns they are accustomed to. An ASD diagnosis is no different. Talking about it, though, can be difficult in the beginning.

Unless you plan on being a public ambassador or champion of autism, telling the world about your diagnosis might not be a good idea. Outside of close friends and family, you should not feel obligated to talk about your ASD diagnosis unless they need to know. This can include co-workers and your boss at work, or other family members you don't have regular contact with.

Before you decide to talk to others about your diagnosis, make sure that you are ready for it. People, particularly family, can have a mix of reactions not dissimilar to the emotions you might have felt when you first received your diagnosis. Depending on their own beliefs, world views, and education, their reaction can be quite different than what you expect. Or, it might be exactly what you might expect if you know them well enough. Be prepared for both positive and negative reactions to your diagnosis. It could go well, or it might hurt. If you think a particular person might not handle the diagnosis well, it might be wise to hold off telling them until you are more comfortable with your diagnosis.

When telling someone about your diagnosis, be prepared to answer some questions about it. Taking some time to learn about ASD and your particular autistic traits can help both you and those you are talking to. Also, try to avoid using too many technical and medical terms that can confuse people. Keep it simple: autism is something you are born with. No two people with autism experience it the same way and at the same levels. Explain how some of your behavior in the past was due to ASD.

Most of all, be patient. Autism can be a tough pill to swallow, even for those who are not diagnosed with it. Like the ripples that form in water after something is dropped in it, an autism diagnosis has the potential of affecting other people's lives. The closer they are to you, the more they will be affected by it. Make sure you take that into consideration before you speak to that person.

Tying It All Together

- Diagnosing someone with ASD should only be done by a professional
- If you think you have autism, there are self-evaluation tests you can find online that can help you determine if you might have autism
- A proper autism diagnosis can only be done by a trained medical professional with experience dealing with ASD
- While there are tests that can be performed to help identify autism, these tests are only part of the full evaluation process
- Autism can be mistaken for other conditions like ADHD, bipolar disorder, and schizophrenia
- ASD can also come with other conditions, like ADHD, epilepsy, OCD, and learning disabilities
- There are a variety of therapies and supportive equipment available for autistic people based on their autistic traits and challenges

- An autism diagnosis, particular if one is not expecting it, can be a very emotional and shocking event in one's life
- Telling others about your ASD diagnosis should be done carefully. You should also expect various reactions, including some you might not anticipate
- Before telling others about your diagnosis, learn about your autism, and be prepared to answer questions about it

CONCLUSION

I couldn't tell you if I had a good childhood or not.
Sure, there were some good times, a lot of them in fact,
but there were also some really bad ones too. I had a
bit of a hard time adjusting to life as I grew older.
Dealing with people was such a hassle that I just
stopped going out, and just stayed in reading. Things
got a little better when I discovered dungeons and
dragons, but still... I wasn't a dumb kid. In fact, I took
a test in grade school that said that I was pretty
smart. But if I didn't like a subject in school, or had a
hard time understanding it, like all of my high school
math classes, it was a miracle if I didn't fail them.
Life as an adult didn't get much easier either. It
pretty much got worse. As a contractor in the IT
industry, being social, and getting along with every-

one, was just as important as your knowledge and skill set. If you didn't fit in, you got the boot. And I got the boot a lot over the years. It fed the narrative in my head that no matter how hard I tried, it would never be good enough, that I would never be what my parents and grandparents envisioned me to be. And that hurt.

I dealt with depression for most of my life, and in my twenties and thirties, it got worse, and came with truckloads of anxiety. I knew there was something wrong with me, but I couldn't figure out what. I tried, I really tried, to get along with everyone, to be the person I was supposed to be. But as soon as I let my guard down, as soon as I got comfortable, the mask would start to slip off, and things would go from bad to disaster real quick.

Finally, when I was thirty-eight, I had a breakdown so bad, it left me with crippling anxiety, to the point where I had panic attacks just by leaving the house to go to the grocery store. It forced me to go see a psychiatrist, and that's when I got my Asperger's diagnosis. I was shocked at first. It took a long while for the implications to sink in. In fact, I'm still trying to get all this, including the smoldering wreckage of my life, back into some semblance of an order. But at least now, I don't worry as much. At least now, I know what's wrong with me, and why I screwed up like I

did in the past, and how I can maybe not repeat
history in the future.
It's a start, one I look forward to, now that I have a
diagnosis, and the help I need.

As we stated at the beginning of the book, autism spectrum disorder is not an illness or a disease that can be cured. It is a developmental spectrum disorder with a variety of traits and challenges of various severities. So much so, that no two people with autism experience it in the same way. So much so, that many people can go years or even decades before being diagnosed.

Autism presents many challenges for those with the disorder. It can sharpen their senses to the point of pain, or dull them to the point of needing to go to the extreme in order to sense anything. It can hinder their ability to socialize with others, can limit the way they think, and prevent them from living normal lives. And in a world made for the neurotypical, the neurodivergent must struggle against a world that does not often accommodate them, or worse, discriminates against them in the form of ableism. Even for people with mild autistic traits and challenges, life is not easy.

But knowledge is power, and hopefully, now that you have reached the end of this book, you have the power to make life for an autistic individual a little easier. You now have a better understanding of what autism is: its symptoms, its traits, and how it can affect an individual. You also know the challenges they face with things like hypersensitivity, black and white thinking, hyperfocus, and all the things that come with them. And more importantly, you also know how to make a difference.

You now know what sensory-friendly environments are and how they can help an autistic person be more comfortable. You know what sensory overload is, and how to help prevent or deal with it when it arises. You understand ableism, and how you can combat it. You've learned ways to help you better communicate with autistic people and to help them overcome some of the daily challenges they face. And while this book might not have taught you everything you need to know, it will have at least put you on the right track, and pointed you in the right direction. So, if you have an autistic person in your life you want to understand and help, now you have some of the tools you need to do so.

Be kind to them. Be patient with them. And be willing to try and see the world through their eyes. Talk to them, understand what their challenges are, and help them overcome them. But don't be their savior. Autistic people don't need a hero to come swooping in to save the day. They need a friend, someone who will treat them like an equal, and will help them when they need it.

We hope this book gave you the answers you were seeking. If they did, leave us a review, tell us what we did right, and maybe share it with others. If not, leave us a review, and tell us what we did wrong. Knowledge is power, but only to those who know it. And to make the world a better place for people with autism, it is the neurotypical that must be informed.

KNOWLEDGE IS POWER

Knowledge is most powerful when it is shared, and now that you have it, you're in a great position to do just that – and you can do so easily.

Simply by sharing your honest opinion of this book and a little about what you've learned, you'll show new readers where they can find all the information they need to improve their understanding of autism and communicate better with the autistic people in their lives.

Thank you for your support. Together, we can help make the world an easier place to live for those with autism.

Scan the QR code to leave a quick review.

REFERENCES

20 Famous People with Autism Spectrum Disorder (ASD) (2021, July 14). Behavioral Innovations. https://behavioral-innovations.com/blog/20-famous-people-with-autism-spectrum-disorder-asd/

Addiction (2021, September). National Autistic Society. https://www.autism.org.uk/advice-and-guidance/topics/mental-health/addiction

Aldoa, A. (2014, August 13). Being Emotionally Flexible. Psychology Today. https://www.psychologytoday.com/us/blog/sweet-emotion/201408/being-emotionally-flexible

Alexithymia (2022, November 21). Wikipedia. https://en.wikipedia.org/wiki/Alexithymia

Anxiety (2021, January). National Autistic Society. https://www.autism.org.uk/advice-and-guidance/topics/mental-health/anxiety

Anxiety and autism (date unknown). Autistica. https://www.autistica.org.uk/what-is-autism/signs-and-symptoms/anxiety-and-autism

Arky, B. (2022, September 16). Why Many Autistic Girls Are Overlooked. Child Mind Institute. https://childmind.org/article/autistic-girls-overlooked-undiagnosed-autism/

Autism Facts & Statistics (2022, July 7). Autism Society Greater Cincinnati. https://www.autismcincy.org/autism-facts-statistics/

Belsky, G. (2022) What is executive function? Understood. https://www.understood.org/en/articles/what-is-executive-function

Bennie, M. (2018, january 19). Executive function: what is it, and how do we support it in those with autism? Part 1. Autism Awareness Centre Inc. https://autismawarenesscentre.com/executive-function-what-is-it-and-how-do-we-support-it-in-those-with-autism-part-i/

Bennie, M. (2020, February 23). Teaching the Concept of Time. Autism Awareness Network Inc. https://autismawarenesscentre.com/teaching-the-concept-of-time/

Bennie, M. (2012, June 8). Who should be told about an autism diagnosis. Autism Awareness Centre Inc. https://autismawarenesscentre.com/told-autism-diagnosis/

Bionexus Health Staff (2020, July 21). 4 Common Feelings After an Autism Diagnosis. Bionexus Health. https://bionexushealth.com/environmental-illness/autism/new-diagnosis/4-common-feelings-after-an-autism-diagnosis/

Bradley, L., Shaw, R., Baron-Cohen, S., Cassidy, S. (2021, December 7). Autistic Adults' Experiences of Camouflaging and Its Perceived Impact on Mental Health. Mary Ann Liebert, Inc. https://www.liebertpub.com/doi/10.1089/aut.2020.0071

Brady, K. (). How Avoiding Conflict Can Cause Problems In Your Relationship. Keir Brady Counseling Services. https://keirbradycounseling.com/avoiding-conflict/

Cariello, C. (2022, April 7) Carrie's Story. Centers for Disease Control and Prevention. https://www.cdc.gov/ncbddd/autism/features/living-with-autism-spectrum-disorder-carrie.html

Casassus, M., Poliakoff, E., Gowen, E., Poole, D., Jones, L.A. (2019, July 23). Time perception and autistic spectrum condition: a systematic review. https://onlinelibrary.wiley.com/doi/full/10.1002/aur.2170

Cognitive Rigidity in Autism (2022). Nurture Pods. https://www.nurturepods.com/cognitive-rigidity-in-autism/

Colorosa, S. (2021, July 22). Top Ways to Approach Time Management on the Spectrum. Autism Parenting Magazine. https://www.autismparentingmagazine.com/autism-time-management/

Communication Tips (2022). National Autism Society. https://www.autism.org.uk/advice-and-guidance/topics/communication/tips

Condo, C.M. (2020, November 19). The Glass Room: Being autistic in a neurotypical world. Neuroclastic. https://neuroclastic.com/the-glass-room-being-autistic-in-a-neurotypical-world/

Cooke, C.E. (2021, August 14). What Is a Sensory-Friendly environment?. Sensory Friendly Solutions. https://www.sensoryfriendly.net/what-is-a-sensory-friendly-environment/

Dattro, L. (2020, May 4). Autistic people may have trouble tuning out distractions. Spectrum. https://www.spectrumnews.org/news/ autistic-people-may-have-trouble-tuning-out-distractions/

Davis, H. (2021). Sharing an Adult Autism Diagnosis with Family and Friends. Adult Autism Center of Lifetime Learning. https://adul tautismcenter.org/blog/sharing-an-adult-autism-diagnosis-with-family-and-friends/

Day# 186 – Interrupters Are Us. (2015, March 13). 366 Days of Autism. https://366daysofautism.wordpress.com/tag/interrupting/

DeAngelis, Z. (2022). 7 Trees That Grow In Freshwater (And Why They Prefer It). Tree Journey. https://treejourney.com/trees-that-grow-in-freshwater-and-why-they-prefer-it/

Denworth, L. (2018, April 19). Social communication in autism, explained. Spectrum. https://www.spectrumnews.org/news/social-communication-autism-explained/

Depression (2021, January). National Autistic Society. https://www. autism.org.uk/advice-and-guidance/topics/mental-health/ depression

Dingwell, R. (2021, June 9). I got diagnosed with autism at 28 years old, and the difficult process changed my life for the better. Insider. https://www.insider.com/diagnosed-with-autism-as-an-adult-experience-2021-6

Douds, M. (2017, February 20). Normal is Relative. Odyssey. https:// www.theodysseyonline.com/normal-is-relative

Dunne, S. (2015, September 16). Autism as an adult: 'On the many days I spend alone I forget how to talk'. The Guardian. https://www. theguardian.com/social-care-network/social-life-blog/2015/sep/ 16/autism-as-an-adult-on-the-many-days-i-spend-alone-i-forget-how-to-talk

Dyspraxia (developmental coordination disorder) in adults. (2020, October 1). NHS. https://www.nhs.uk/conditions/developmental-coordination-disorder-dyspraxia-in-adults/

Egber, M. (2021, April 6) 30 Quotes from 30 People with Autism. Els for Autism. https://www.elsforautism.org/30-quotes-from-30-people-with-autism/

Eisenmenger, A. (2019, December 12). Ableism 101. Access Living. https://www.accessliving.org/newsroom/blog/ableism-101/

Emily (April 10). Hypo and Hyper Sensitivity in Autistic People. Authentically Emily. https://www.authenticallyemily.uk/blog/hypo-and-hyper-sensitivity-in-autistic-people

Eugenics (2022, December 11). Wikipedia. https://en.wikipedia.org/wiki/Eugenics

Eugenics and Scientific Racism (2022, May 18). National Human Genome Research Institute. https://www.genome.gov/about-genomics/fact-sheets/Eugenics-and-Scientific-Racism

Executive Function (2022). Autism Speaks. https://www.autismspeaks.org/executive-functioning

Fitzgerald, R. (2022). A Homeowner's Guide to Creating A Sensory-Friendly Space For Individuals with Sensory Processing Disorders. Uphomes. https://uphomes.com/blog/homeowners-guide-creating-sensory-friendly-space/

Flynn, J. (2018, January 18). 10 Struggles Being Neurodiverse in a Neurotypical World. The Mighty. https://themighty.com/topic/autism-spectrum-disorder/being-neurodiverse-in-a-neurotypical-world/

Frances, N. (2016, June 1). ASD Black or White Thinking Style. Linkedin. https://www.linkedin.com/pulse/asd-black-white-thinking-style-nelle-frances

Frye, D. (2021, April 28). What Do Language Processing Disorders Look Like in Adults? Additude. https://www.additudemag.com/language-disorders-in-adults-symptoms-and-treatment/

Garcia, A. (2019, April 18). Read This If You Don't Know How to Talk to Someone Who Has Autism. Healthline. https://www.healthline.com/health/autism/dear-neurotypical-guide-to-autism#First,-lets-start-with-definitions

Gaig, S. (2014, April 7). People with autism don't lack emotions but often have difficulty identifying them. The Conversation. https://theconversation.com/people-with-autism-dont-lack-emotions-but-often-have-difficulty-identifying-them-25225

Gil, S., Chambres, P., Hyvert, C., Fanget, M., Droit-Violet, S. (2012,

November 21). Children with Autism Spectrum Disorders Have "The Working Raw Material" for Time Perception. Plos One. https://journals.plos.org/plosone/article?id=10.1371/journal.pone.0049116

Glossary of Autism Spectrum Disorders related Terminology (2022). Easterseals. https://www.easterseals.com/support-and-education/living-with-autism/glossary-of-autism-disorders.html

Greutman, H. (2015, June 11). What are the 8 Senses?. Growing Hands-On Kids. https://www.growinghandsonkids.com/what-are-the-8-senses.html

Grinspoon, P. (2022, May 4). How to recognize and tame your cognitive distortions. Harvard Health Publishing. https://www.health.harvard.edu/blog/how-to-recognize-and-tame-your-cognitive-distortions-202205042738

Hall, M.J. (2022, November 4). What Is Kanner Syndrome. Wisegeek. https://www.wise-geek.com/what-is-kanner-syndrome.htm

Ham, H. (2022). What You Need To Understand About Attention and Cognitive Fatigue in Adults On The Autism Spectrum. Spectrum Fusion. https://spectrumfusion.org/2018/05/attention-and-cognitive-fatigue-in-adults-on-the-autism-spectrum/

Hull, L., Mandy, W. (2019, November 27). Camouflaging in Autism. Frontiers for Young Minds. https://kids.frontiersin.org/articles/10.3389/frym.2019.00129

Is handedness determined by genetics? (2022, July 8). Medicine Plus. https://medlineplus.gov/genetics/understanding/traits/handedness/

Jekel, D. (2022). Climbing Out From Under the To-Do List. Asperger/Autism Network. https://www.aane.org/climbing-out-from-under-the-to-do-list/

Jones, L. (2008, December 19). What is Normal? Serendip Studios. https://serendipstudio.org/exchange/ljones/what-normal

Jumping to Conclusions: Learn How To Stop Making Anxiety-Fueled Mental Leaps (2020, December 30). Therapy Now SF. https://www.therapynowsf.com/blog/jumping-to-conclusions-learn-how-to-stop-making-anxiety-fueled-mental-leaps

Hartney, E. (2022, November 15). 10 Cognitive Distortions That Can Cause Negative Thinking. Verywell Mind. https://www.verywell mind.com/ten-cognitive-distortions-identified-in-cbt-22412

Hare, J. (2020, October 26). My autism diagnosis: grieving for the version of my younger self. Ambitious About Autism. https://www. ambitiousaboutautism.org.uk/about-us/media-centre/blog/griev ing-for-version-of-my-younger-self

Healis Autism Centre (March 29). How Receptive Language Builds The Way to Successful Communication for Children with Autism. Healis Autism Centre. https://www.healisautism.com/post/recep tive-language-builds-way-successful-communication-children-autism

How to Get Tested for Autism as an Adult (2014, July 25). Autism Speaks. https://www.autismspeaks.org/expert-opinion/getting-evaluated-autism-adult-where-go-who-see

Impulsivity (2022, September 7). Wikipedia. https://en.wikipedia.org/ w/index.php?title=Impulsivity&action=history

Keelan, P. (date unknown). Emotional Reasoning: A cognitive distortion with powerful effects. Dr. Patrick Keelan. https://drpatrickkee lan.com/anxiety/emotional-reasoning-a-cognitive-distortion-with-powerful-effects/

Key Findings: CDC Releases First Estimates of the Number of Adults Living with Autism Spectrum Disorder in the United States (2022, April 17). Centers for Disease Control and Prevention. https:// www.cdc.gov/ncbddd/autism/features/adults-living-with-autism-spectrum-disorder.html

Kent, R., Smimonoff, E. (2017). Chapter 2 – Prevalence of Anxiety in Autism Spectrum Disorders. Science Direct. https://www.sciencedi rect.com/science/article/pii/B9780128051221000028

Khan, T. (2022, February 14). Sophie's Story. Autism Unlimited. https://www.autism-unlimited.org/blog/sophias-story/

Koydemir, S. (date unknown). Emotional flexibility is the key to well-being. Selda Koydemir. https://www.seldakoydemir.com/ resources/emotional-flexibility-is-the-key-to-wellbeing

Late Diagnosis: Stories About Being Diagnosed As An Adult (2019,

November 8). The Story Collider. https://www.storycollider.org/ stories/2019/11/5/late-diagnosis-stories-about-being-diagnosed-as-an-adult

Let's Design Your Site (2021, August 28). Meltdowns and overstimulation versus temper tantrums and outbursts of anger. Advocating Autism Spectrum Talents Through Self Discovery & Social Education. https://www.onthespectrumfoundation.org/post/melt-downs-and-overstimulation-versus-temper-tantrums-and-outbursts-of-anger

Lingle, J. (2022, June 15). What To Say Instead of No! Autism Educates. https://www.autismeducates.com/2012/06/15/what-to-say-instead-of-no/

Loftus, Y. (2021, October 8). Hyposensitivity Among Autistic Individuals. Autism parenting Magazine. https://www.autismpar entingmagazine.com/hyposensitivity-among-autistic-individuals/

Maguire, C. (2021, October). Coping with Sensory Overload. ADHD Newsstand. https://chadd.org/adhd-news/adhd-news-adults/ coping-with-sensory-overload/

Mascarelli, M.L. (2010, September 20). Timer perception problems may explain autism symptoms. Spectrum. https://www.spectrum news.org/news/time-perception-problems-may-explain-autism-symptoms/

Matusiak, M. (2022). How to create an autism-friendly environment. Living Autism. https://livingautism.com/create-autism-friendly-environment/

Mayo Clinic Staff. (2022, May 3). Rett Syndrome. Mayo Clinic. https:// www.mayoclinic.org/diseases-conditions/rett-syndrome/symp toms-causes/syc-20377227

Meester, A., Vancleef, L.M.G., Peters, M.L. (2018, December 20). Emotional flexibility and recovery from pain. Springer Link. https://link.springer.com/article/10.1007/s11031-018-9748-5

MGH News and Public Affairs (2022, January 25). Study explores possible autism link in young adults treated for addiction. The Harvard Gazette. https://news.harvard.edu/gazette/story/2022/ 01/study-explores-autism-link-in-teens-treated-for-addiction/

Miller, L. (2021, June 15). What is cognitive flexibility, and why does it matter? BetterUp. https://lifeskillsadvocate.com/blog/hyperfixa tions-adhd-what-you-need-to-know/

Monaco, C. (2021, January 4). Untreated Autism Spectrum Disorder Tied to Alcohol, Drug Abuse. Medpage Today. https://www. medpagetoday.com/pediatrics/autism/90517

Moss, J. (2022, November 1). Why it's important to stretch and improve your emotional flexibility: Jeninifer Moss. CBC News. https://www.cbc.ca/news/canada/kitchener-waterloo/happiness-column-jennifer-moss-emotional-flexibility-1.5781721

Mulder, J. (2020, April 23). How to Deal with Sensory Overload: 19 Coping Strategies. The Health Sessions. https://thehealthsessions. com/how-to-deal-with-sensory-overload/

McArthur, A. (2022, May 10). Struggle With Task paralysis? Here's What It Is – and How to Overcome It. Sweety High. https://www. sweetyhigh.com/read/what-is-task-paralysis-and-how-to-over come-it-051022

Morey, E. (2022) Autism and Impulse Control: What You Need to Know. The Autism Site News. https://blog.theautismsite.greater good.com/impulse-control/

National Institute of Mental Health (March 2022). Autism Spectrum Disorder. National Institute of Mental Health. https://www.nimh. nih.gov/health/topics/autism-spectrum-disorders-asd

National Institute of Mental Health (2022, May). Post-Traumatic Stress Disorder. National Institute of Mental Health. https://www.nimh. nih.gov/health/topics/post-traumatic-stress-disorder-ptsd

Nerenburg, J. (2020, March 27). How to Deal with Sensory Overload as a Sensitive Person. Greater Good Magazine. https://greatergood. berkeley.edu/article/item/ how_to_deal_with_sensory_overload_as_a_sensitive_person

Neurodivergent (2022, February 6). Cleveland Clinic. https://my.cleve landclinic.org/health/symptoms/23154-neurodivergent

Nield, D. (2020, August 9). Why Are Only 10% of People Left-Handed? Here's What Scientists Know So Far. Science Alert. https://www.

sciencealert.com/why-are-only-10-of-people-left-handed-here-s-what-scientists-know-so-far

Nightingale121 (2018, June 1). Executive Function and Choice Paralysis. Autism Forums. https://www.autismforums.com/blogs/executive-function-and-choice-paralysis.2771/

Other conditions that affect autistic people (2022, October 4). NHS. https://www.nhs.uk/conditions/autism/other-conditions/

Overview – Dyslexia. (2022, March 7). NHS. https://www.nhs.uk/conditions/dyslexia/

Overview – Epilepsy. (2020, September 18). NHS. https://www.nhs.uk/conditions/epilepsy/

Overview – Learning Disabilities. (2022, January 10). NHS. https://www.nhs.uk/conditions/learning-disabilities/

Overview – Obsessive compulsive disorder (OCD) (2019, November 18). NHS. https://www.nhs.uk/mental-health/conditions/obsessive-compulsive-disorder-ocd/overview/

Oskerova, J. (202, March 5). 3 Types of Flexibility. Linkedin. https://www.linkedin.com/pulse/3-types-flexibility-mgr-jarmila-oskerova-celta

Paeds in a pod (2021, August 16). Sensory processing and our 8 senses explained (yes, 8, not 5!). Paeds in a pod. https://www.paedsinapod.com.au/sensory-processing-and-our-8-senses-explained-yes-8-not-5/

Prakhartrivedi (2021, August 7). 5 Reasons Why Expressive Language Is Important For Us. Icy Tales. https://icytales.com/5-reasons-why-expressive-language-is-important/

Personalization: A Common Type of Negative Thinking. Therapy Now SF. https://www.therapynowsf.com/blog/personalization-a-common-type-of-negative-thinking

Pervasive Developmental Disorder – Not Otherwise Specified (PDD-NOS). (2022). Autism Speaks. https://www.autismspeaks.org/pervasive-developmental-disorder-pdd-nos

Petrides, K.V., Mandy, W. (2020, January 29). The Female Autism Phenotype and Camouflaging: A Narrative Review. Springer Link. https://link.springer.com/article/10.1007/s40489-020-00197-9

Pierce, R. (2022). Hyperfixation & ADHD: What You Need To Know. Like Skills Advocate. https://lifeskillsadvocate.com/blog/hyperfixations-adhd-what-you-need-to-know/

Ploszajski, A. (2019, September 13). Women 'better than men at disguising autism symptoms'. The Guardian. https://www.theguardian.com/society/2019/sep/13/women-better-than-men-at-disguising-autism-symptoms

Powell, P. (2019, May 6). I finally understood why I felt different after my autism diagnosis. Autism Speaks. https://www.autismspeaks.org/life-spectrum/i-finally-understood-why-i-felt-different-after-my-autism-diagnosis

Receptive and Expressive Language Disorders (2022). University of Washington. https://sphsc.washington.edu/receptive-and-expressive-language-disorders

Resnick, A. (2022, October 24). What Does It Mean to Be Neurotypical?. Verywell Mind. https://www.verywellmind.com/what-does-it-mean-to-be-neurotypical-5195919

Resnick, A. (2022, July 21). What Is Neurodivergence and What Does It Mean to Be Neurodivergent? Verywell Health. https://www.verywellmind.com/what-is-neurodivergence-and-what-does-it-mean-to-be-neurodivergent-5196627

Rett Syndrome. (2021) Nord. https://rarediseases.org/rare-diseases/rett-syndrome/

Roberts, E. (2017, June 15). Cognitive Flexibility: Keeping thinking limber and flexible. Organization for Autism Research. https://researchautism.org/cognitive-flexibility-keeping-thinking-limber-and-flexible/

Rowland, J. (2019, May 24). Through my eyes: High Functioning autism. Medical News Today. https://www.medicalnewstoday.com/articles/325239

Rudy, L.J. (2022, July 16). Sensory Overload in Autism. Verywell Health. https://www.verywellhealth.com/autism-and-sensory-overload-259892

Rudy, L.J. (2022, August 27). What Does "Neurotypical" Mean?

Verywell Health. https://www.verywellhealth.com/what-does-it-mean-to-be-neurotypical-260047

Rumball, F. (2022, March 30). Post-traumatic stress disorder in autistic people. National Autism Society. https://www.autism.org.uk/advice-and-guidance/professional-practice/ptsd-autism

Russo, F. (2018, February 21). The costs of camouflaging autism. Spectrum. https://www.spectrumnews.org/features/deep-dive/costs-camouflaging-autism/

Sarris, M. (2022, March 24). Autism, Meltdowns, and the Struggle to Manage Emotions. Spark. https://sparkforautism.org/discover_article/managing-emotions/

Salters-Pedneault, K. (2020, July 10). What Is Impulsivity? Verywell Mind. https://www.verywellmind.com/impulsive-behavior-and-bpd-425483

Sardella, A., Vittorio, L., Bonanno, G.A., Basile, G., Quattropani, M.C. (2021, February 10). Expressive Flexibility and Dispositional Optimism Contribute to the Elderly's Resilience and Health-Related Quality of Life during the COVID-19 Pandemic. National Library of Medicine. https://www.ncbi.nlm.nih.gov/pmc/articles/PMC7916547/

Sensory Overload in Autism: Sensitivity Differences (2021, December 14). Otsimo. https://otsimo.com/en/sensory-overload-autism/

Sheikh, H. (2022, November 8). How is Adult Autism Diagnosed. Verywell Health. https://www.verywellhealth.com/diagnosing-autism-or-asperger-syndrome-in-adults-259946

Silvertant, M. (2020, November 29). Autism & Camouflaging. Embrace Autism. https://embrace-autism.com/autism-and-camouflaging/

Slattery, A., Castle, B. (2021, February 5). Ableism in the Workplace: What it is & How to Combat It. Inhersight. https://www.inhersight.com/blog/guides-to-discrimination/ableism

Sleep – a guide for autistic adults (2020, August 14). National Autistic Society. https://www.autism.org.uk/advice-and-guidance/topics/physical-health/sleep/autistic-adults

Social Communication (date unknown). Autism Tasmania. https://

www.autismtas.org.au/about-autism/key-areas-of-difference/
social-communication-differences/

Spencer, A.L. (2021, December 4). How to make a Visual Schedule for Autism. The Autistic Innovator Shop. https://shop.autisticinnova
tor.com/blogs/the-autistic-innovator/how-to-make-a-visual-sched
ule-for-autism

Star, K. (2020, April 23). Cognitive Distortions of Magnification and Minimization. Verywell Mind. https://www.verywellmind.com/
magnification-and-minimization-2584183

Stimming. (2022, November 21). Wikipedia. https://en.wikipedia.org/
wiki/Stimming

Talking about a diagnosis (2021). Autism Awareness Australia. https://
www.autismawareness.com.au/diagnosis/adults/talking-about-a-
diagnosis

Tatum, E. (2013, October 4). 10 Ways to Avoid Everyday Ableism. Everyday Feminism. https://everydayfeminism.com/2013/10/
avoid-everyday-ableism/

The Facts About Autism in American Adults (2022). University of Maryland Medical System. https://health.umms.org/2022/03/25/
adults-and-autism/

The Teacher's Guide to Combating Classroom Ableism (date unknown). Planbook. https://blog.planbook.com/classroom-ableism/

Therapy and Assistive Technology (2022). AASPIRE Healthcare Toolkit. https://autismandhealth.org/?a=pt&p=detail&t=pt_aut&s=
aut_ther&theme=lt&

Tidy, C. (2021, January 25). Childhood Disintegrative Disorder. Patient. https://patient.info/doctor/childhood-disintegrative-disor
der-hellers-syndrome

Time Management on the Autism Spectrum (2018, December 9). Life With Aspergers. https://life-with-aspergers.blogspot.com/2018/
12/time-management-on-autism-spectrum.html

Tobik, A. (2021, August 5). *Quotes about autism*. Autism Parenting Magazine. https://www.autismparentingmagazine.com/quotes-
about-autism/

Unhelpful Thinking Styles (date unknown). Autistica. https://www.autistica.org.uk/what-is-autism/anxiety-and-autism-hub/unhelpful-thinking-styles

United We Care (2021, September 21). Hyperfixation vs. Hyperfocus: ADHD, Autism, and Mental Illness. United We Care. https://www.unitedwecare.com/hyperfixation-vs-hyperfocus/

Uniyal, P. (2022, July 5). What is task paralysis and how to beat it; psychotherapist offers tips. Hindustan Times. https://www.hindustantimes.com/lifestyle/health/what-is-task-paralysis-and-how-to-beat-it-psychologist-offers-tips-101658739785498.html

Villines, Z. (2021, November 7). What is ableism, and what is its impact? Medical News Today. https://www.medicalnewstoday.com/articles/ableism#impact

Voyles Askham, A. (2020, October 15). Brain structure changes in autism, explained. Spectrum. https://www.spectrumnews.org/news/brain-structure-changes-in-autism-explained/

Wallace, A. (2020, May 16). The Difference Between Receptive and Expressive Language. NAPA. https://napacenter.org/receptive-vs-expressive-language/

Wallace-Ilse, H. (date unknown). Why do Autistic People Take Things Literally? The Ringmaster's Tale. https://autism-all-stars.org/autistic-literal-thinking/

Watts, C. (2022, May 23). What is Autistic Masking? High Speed Training. https://www.highspeedtraining.co.uk/hub/what-is-autistic-masking/

Weingarten, R. (2019, August 29). Finish What You Started: How to Avoid Task Paralysis. Clear Voice. https://www.clearvoice.com/blog/task-paralysis/

What is Asperger's Syndrome? (2022). Nationwide Children's. https://www.nationwidechildrens.org/conditions/aspergers-syndrome

What is the relationship Between Autism and Impulse Control? (2022). AppliedBehaviorAnalysisEdu.org. https://www.appliedbehavioranalysisedu.org/what-is-the-relationship-between-autism-and-impulse-control/

Wigmore, I. (2022) Time Management. Whatis.com. https://www.techtarget.com/whatis/definition/time-management

Weinstock, C.P. (2019, July 31). The deep emotional ties between depression and autism. Spectrum. https://www.spectrumnews.org/features/deep-dive/the-deep-emotional-ties-between-depression-and-autism/

White, S. (2014, June 20). Effective adaptability – how can you become a better leader? 20th Air Force. https://www.20af.af.mil/News/Commentaries/Display/Article/825848/effective-adaptabilityhow-can-you-become-a-better-leader/

Wilkinson, L.A. (2022). Decision-Making Problems in Adults with ASD. Living Autism. https://livingautism.com/decision-making-problems-adults-asd/

Yerys, B.E. (2022, August 12). Q: How Can I Get Evaluated for Autism as an Adult? Additude. https://www.additudemag.com/how-to-get-tested-for-autism-adult-diagnosis/

Your 8 Senses (2022). Star Institute. https://www.autism-unlimited.org/blog/sophias-story/

Printed in Great Britain
by Amazon

35649069R00106